SELL
YOUR WAY
TO THE TOP

Sound Wisdom Books by Zig Ziglar

A View from the Top

A View from the Top Action Guide

Goals—How to Get the Most Out of Your Life

Sell Your Way to the Top—Proven Principles for Successful Selling

You're a Natural Champion—Allow Your Self-Esteem & Positive Mindset to Shine

ZIG ZIGLAR

SELL YOUR WAY TO THE TOP

PROVEN PRINCIPLES FOR SUCCESSFUL SELLING

Published and distributed by:
SOUND WISDOM
P.O. Box 310
Shippensburg, PA 17257-0310
717-530-2122

info@soundwisdom.com

www.soundwisdom.com

While efforts have been made to verify information contained in this
publication, neither the author nor the publisher assumes any responsibility
for errors, inaccuracies, or omissions. While this publication is chock-full
of useful, practical information; it is not intended to be legal or accounting
advice. All readers are advised to seek competent lawyers and accountants
to follow laws and regulations that may apply to specific situations.
The reader of this publication assumes responsibility for the use of the
information. The author and publisher assume no responsibility or liability
whatsoever on the behalf of the reader of this publication.

Cover/jacket design by Eileen Rockwell

ISBN 13 TP: 978-1-64095-335-2

ISBN 13 eBook: 978-1-64095-336-9

For Worldwide Distribution, Printed in the U.S.A.

1 2 3 4 5 6 7 8 / 26 25 24 23 22

CONTENTS

INTRODUCTION

When you think about selling, you think about success. And when you think about successful selling, there is one name that has been synonymous with that term for more than 50 years—Zig Ziglar. The mere mention of his name, even now, years after his passing, opens doors and sales organizations worldwide because serious businesses know of his acumen.

When it comes to selling and motivation, Zig Ziglar did it all, and you are about to read one of the most exciting aspects of his years of wisdom—perhaps leading to the most valuable experiences of your selling career. Zig reveals how to *sell your way to the top.*

In this book, Zig shares with you his proven principles for successful selling. These simple yet proven successful and effective strategies will help make all your sales calls more profitable. His practical suggestions can be used immediately to increase your efficiency—and turn you into a top sales professional.

Zig's enthusiasm, understanding, and ability to communicate with people of all ages made him one of the most widely read and listened to motivators in the United States. He founded the Zig Ziglar Corporation, a multinational training company based in Dallas, Texas, in 1977. Zig regularly toured the US and Canada presenting his inspiring messages to a variety of groups and organization—influencing an estimated quarter of a billion individuals through his 74, and now 75, books.

Zig challenges and motivates you to learn the skills to help you close the sale today as you build customers and a career for tomorrow.

Get ready!

You're about to receive positive advice about real-world successes—revealing conclusively that these strategies work! This book contains step-by-step instructions showing you exactly how to sell your product or service.

Success =
Opportunity + Preparation

It's been said that "Failure is the line of least resistance." Also said is, "Success occurs when opportunity meets preparation." I believe both are true statements. You can start receiving the rewards, the dreams, and the desires you've always wanted. Setting goals works. With Zig Ziglar as your teacher, you can't help but achieve every goal and sell your way to the top!

You will discover:

- How to think like a seller *and* a buyer for tremendous results.

- How honesty and kindness equal sales.

- The power of positive projection.

- How to use your verbal paintbrush to set the scene.

- Why questions are so very important to making the sale.

- The secrets to specific, tried and true, closes— that work!

Success is worth the time and effort, but it's not enough to sustain a lifetime at the top. After success, the next step is to *move from success to significance.* Achieving your sales goals will persuade you to commit to being the best you can be and convince you to recognize and continue to develop what you already have, what you can and will do—ultimately striving to help others get what they need and want.

Whether you are just now experiencing Zig Ziglar for the first time or even if you have followed him for years, this book will be a life-changing revelation.

CHAPTER 1

TWENTY-FIVE SALES POINTS

In November 1975, I was in the market for a new automobile. I had looked at a couple of Cadillacs and fell in love with them. I thought that the '76 model was really sharp.

A few days later I was talking to a good buddy of mine, telling him that I was looking at Cadillacs and he said, "Man, until you've talked with Chuck, you're behind the times. Go see him, he'll really treat you right."

"Well," I said, "I don't know Chuck and he's a buddy of yours. How about you call him and I'll be on my way over there while you're talking to him."

"Consider it done," he said.

When I pulled into the only open parking spot in the lot, there stood Chuck. And even though I didn't know him until then, I knew it was him because of his appearance, the way he was raised, and the description I'd been given—very conservative, neatly attired.

As I turned off the motor, Chuck literally opened the door for me and said, "You've got to be Zig Ziglar."

"Yes, I am."

He was a very formal guy, so he said, "Well, Mr. Ziglar, let me tell you how glad I am to meet you. And I want to also say before I say anything else, this is truly a beautiful automobile you're driving."

And it really was. It was a Regency Oldsmobile, fully loaded, chocolate brown, and in great condition. So, he was paying me a sincere compliment.

Sales Point #1: Offer a sincere compliment.

That's the first sales point I would like to make. A sincere compliment is a good way to start a presentation. Now the obvious key word is *sincere*. If I'd been driving a dog and he said something like that, I'd have grabbed my wallet and run.

Sales Point #2: Make the prospect feel good about a previous purchase.

His comment has a second sales point before we even get out of the gates. And that is, the best way to make a new sale is to make the prospect feel good about a previous purchase.

Then Chuck said to me, "Zig, do you mind telling me where you bought this car?"

"Well, as a matter of fact, my neighbor who lives across the street is an executive with General Motors, and he made arrangements for me to get a car through one of their dealers."

"Well, let me ask you, did you, by any chance, get one of the executive cars?"

Sales Point #3: A sales professional asks a lot of questions.

Now here's sales point number three: To be really successful, a sales professional will ask an awful lot of questions. To get important background information from people, ask them questions.

Sales Point #4: The prospect will give you pertinent information.

And that brings us to sales point number four: The prospect will give you pertinent information if you just ask.

Chuck walked around the car a time or two looking it over, and then he said, "It's absolutely gorgeous. Let me get the appraiser and he'll give it a look. And I'm going to tell you one thing, Mr. Ziglar, if this car of yours is as nice on the inside as it is on the outside, we're going to be able to swap and make you happy because we have such beautiful inventory."

The appraiser appeared and he and Chuck drove the car to wherever it is they go to do whatever it is they do for an appraisal. I looked around the lot while I was waiting for them to return. I want to emphasize that the optimism Chuck displayed represents point number five, which is salespeople should be optimistic.

Sales Point #5: Salespeople should be optimistic.

Chuck said my car was nice, he had a beautiful inventory to work from, and he initially gave me hope. That's what I wanted. He gave me hope that we were going to make a trade.

When they returned, as they pulled into the parking lot, I could see Chuck had a big smile on his face. And I thought to myself, *Hey, he really likes my car.* And then, I have to confess to you, a thought ran through my mind. Now I didn't let it stay long, but it entered my mind that since he liked my car so much, I was going to be able to steal this deal. I even got to thinking maybe he was even going to pay *me* to swap since he loved my car as much as he did.

Let me emphasize the point that I was thinking like a buyer. And that's what I'm supposed to do because I was buying. But sales point number six is this: To succeed in selling, you, the salesperson, must sit on both sides of the table. You have to think as a buyer and you also have to think as a seller.

Sales Point #6: A salesperson must think as a buyer AND as a seller.

When Chuck stepped out of my car, he was grinning so wide he could eat a banana sideways. I had never seen anything quite like it. After he stepped out of the car, he closed the door. And then like he couldn't believe it, he opened the door and closed it again. As he was shaking his head, he said, "Mr. Ziglar, this car of yours is even nicer on the inside than it is on the outside. As matter of fact, I'm delighted you're here. But I'm a little puzzled, Mr. Ziglar. Why would you want to trade in this gorgeous automobile right now?"

That was a powerful and positive comment for Chuck to make.

You might be thinking, *Well, gee, why would he bring up something like that at this point? You're in there, you want to trade. What business is that of his why you want to trade? What difference does it make to him why you want to swap now?* To that I say, Chuck's question is one of the strongest points in this entire sales experience and an important lesson to learn up front.

Sales Point #7: Sell on the offense—not the defense.

Sales point number seven: If there's anything wrong, if there are any questions, if there are any objections, it is better to deal with them early in the sales presentation instead of later on as a rebuttal. This way you can sell on the offense, not on the defense.

"Why do you want to swap right now?" Chuck asked.

I kind of smiled and said, "Well, Chuck, we have a family reunion over in Mississippi, and I think it'd kind of be nice to drive a new Cadillac over there."

At that point, Chuck got out what I call a "talking pad"—a tool that all professional salespeople must have. He was holding a tablet of some kind and while he was talking, he was also figuring. The reason for this is very simple. In our society, we have been conditioned to "believe what we see and doubt what we hear." All of our lives we have heard the statement, "You can't always believe everything you hear." But all of our lives we also have heard, "Listen, I saw it with my own two eyes, and seeing is believing." Absolutely.

Sales Point #8: Prospects buy only when they believe and/or understand.

So sales point number eight: Prospects buy only when they believe and/or understand. Consequently, when you write down the numbers, the chance of the person believing and understanding is much greater.

Now here's a very significant point—Chuck is selling me both logically and emotionally. If you use all logic in a presentation, you'll have the best educated prospect in town who can go down the street and buy something from someone else. On the other hand, if you use all emotion in the presentation, people get emotionally involved and buy, but then they might cancel the transaction the next day or the next week.

Tie the two together—logic and emotion—and the prospects will buy logically today, seeing to believe, combined with emotion, being moved by the tone and words of your voice. Consequently, you are building a successful career in sales.

With another big smile, Chuck got his pad out and started figuring. Obviously I was watching him carefully because I'm deeply involved in this deal. After he'd been figuring a minute, his smile began to fade. And as I watched that smile disappear, my heart started to sink a little bit and I thought, *Oh no, he's finding something wrong and I'm not going to get that beautiful automobile.*

Chuck kept thinking and his neutral expression changed from bland into ugly. As a matter of fact, I have never seen such a high concentration of ugly in one spot in my lifetime as Chuck was displaying right then.

As my heart sank a little more, I just stood there not knowing what to do. But I'll give Chuck credit for one thing, he's a fighter. He stayed right in there and figured and figured and figured. And pretty soon that ugly disappeared and his expression moved back into neutral. And I caught myself pulling for him, *Hang in there, Chuck. Stay with it, boy. Man, stay with it, stay with it.* And I'll tell you, he hung in there all the way.

Finally he looked up at me with a huge smile on his face. Showing me the pad, he said, "Mr. Ziglar, the good news to you is that because of our wonderful inventory and because of the marvelous condition of your automobile, we can swap with you for just $7,385."

When he said that, I screamed like a stuck pig, "Whoa, Chuck! Man, that's a lot of money!" I almost had a heart attack when he said it.

He looked at me with a half-smile and said, "Mr. Ziglar, is it too much?"

Right away I thought, *What's he saying to me? Is he saying, "Man, Ziglar, if that's out of your price range, if you can't handle that kind of money, be a man about it, admit it. Just say you can't cut it."*

Now, do you think for one moment, I would say or ever admit to a thing like that? There ain't no way.

Sales Point #9: Ask, "Is it too much?"

But sales point number nine is when you use the right voice inflection and ask, "Is it too much?" which makes the buyer think about two very important questions: *Am I being asked if it's out of my price range? That's one thing. Or am I being asked, "Mr. Ziglar, as a wise and prudent businessman, is $7,385 more than you're willing to pay?"* Well, as a wise and prudent businessman, I plead guilty to that last one.

So I responded, "Chuck, that's simply more money than I'm going to pay you for a difference in these two cars."

He didn't argue with me; he didn't get defensive; he didn't try to justify the price. With an almost casual confidence, Chuck looked at me as he put the ball back my court. And that's, after all, where the decision is ultimately going to be made.

Sales Point #10: Don't argue. Toss the ball back to the prospect.

Sales point number 10 is this: Don't argue. Don't get defensive or try to justify the price at that point. Give the ball back to the prospect. So, pleasantly and gently, Chuck stayed on the offense and said, "Mr. Ziglar, what do you think would be a fair exchange between your nice, clean, four-year-old Regency Oldsmobile, and our gorgeous new Cadillac sedan DeVille?"

Sales Point #11: Politely compare the two products.

Sales point number 11: Use the Abraham Lincoln approach. That's what Chuck was doing. It's been told that when Abraham Lincoln was a courtroom attorney, at times he would represent both sides of the case, saying good things about the opposition. As a matter of fact, sometimes Abe had a better case for the other side. But he obviously saved the most eloquent statements for his own client.

Notice what Chuck did. He mentioned good things about my previous purchase, the Oldsmobile, but had more eloquent compliments about his own product, the Cadillac. And that's what you need to do. Chuck described a "nice, clean, four-year-old Oldsmobile Regency" compared to his "gorgeous new Cadillac sedan DeVille," emphasizing "gorgeous new Cadillac." I could even feel the difference between the two vehicles.

Sales Point #12: Defend the prospect's previous purchase.

So, sales point number 12 is to defend the prospect's previous purchase.

At this point, even if the prospect says ugly things about the previous purchase, you must be guarded in your answer. For example, if the prospect says, "Man, when I got this, they saw me coming and really took advantage of me." If you agree, the prospect may think, *Yeah, that last dude got me, but I'll guarantee* **you're** *not going to swindle me.*

Sales Point #13: Determine if the person is a serious prospect.

So, now we are at sales point number 13. Chuck had now invested about 25 minutes with me. At this point, as a professional he needs to determine if I am a legitimate prospect or not. Spending 25 minutes is fine, but you can't really invest that much time with everybody if they aren't going to be prospects. You need to find out if you're in the same ballpark or if you're in different ballgames.

Now I literally reached over and took the talking pad out of Chuck's hand and said to him, "Chuck, I've always believed in round figures and I believe that $7,000 would be plenty to pay for that car in exchange, and that includes the tax and all the other charges."

Chuck calmly, quietly, and seriously said, "Mr. Ziglar, you asked the impossible. You're asking for a $385 discount. The taxes on it would be $350 at $735. There's not a chance in a million that our company would go along with your offer."

Notice he said, "Your offer."

But then Chuck said, "But in the unlikely event they should be prepared to accept your offer, are you prepared to drive this beautiful, new Cadillac sedan DeVille home with you?"

Now all of a sudden it occurred to me that this guy is serious about selling. And it also occurred to me that if somebody didn't do something, somebody is about to buy something. And that guy didn't even know what I was selling.

Many times when you've made an offer or you made an offer to accept an offer, at that point a lot of people start to crawfish. That's exactly what I did. I said, "I don't know about that, Chuck. I mean, seven thousand dollars is a lot of money, and my money doesn't come in that easy." Then my doubts entered the picture, *Do I really want a Cadillac? Do I want a green one? Do I want a sedan DeVille?*

Sales Point #14: Integrity is key.

And here's what a sales expert says, as we make sales point number 14. Sales expert Charles Roth says that at major decision time, the prospect is temporarily insane. They are so excited or confused or puzzled, they don't know what to do. And so at this point, the kind of *person* you are is infinitely more important than the kind of *salesperson* you are. Your integrity is so important; because if the prospect doesn't trust you, he or she won't buy from you.

And let me emphasize a point here. Chuck had been working on me for more than twenty years to sell me this car. Oh, I know I said earlier that I had just met him—and I did just meet him. But Chuck had been working on me for two decades, because twenty years earlier he started selling Cadillac automobiles. Twenty years earlier he had decided, "I'm going to make my career doing exactly this." And he knew that the only way he could build a career would be to deal right off the top of the deck—no unethical dealings. Subsequently, he had an incredibly high percentage of repeat business.

Sales Point #15: Develop professional sales skills.

Sales point number 15—the right kind of person in sales will train and study to develop professional sales skills. That's what Chuck had been doing.

Let's look at the sales skills Chuck developed.

I had taken his talking pad and wrote $7,000 as my offer. He reached for the pad and then he scratched out that $7,000 and he said, "Mr. Ziglar, I don't think there's a chance our company would go along with that offer. Let's look at the $7,385. I know we'll go along with that offer because we've already made it." Then he smiled so gently and said, "And Mr. Ziglar, we don't back out on our offers."

Sales Point #16: Be confidently serious.

Sales point number 16 is this. Chuck was communicating a very important message to me. He was saying, "Mr. Ziglar, I'm not playing games with you. I'm serious about negotiating and I expect you to be serious too." At this point, he went back to his talking pad. "Mr. Ziglar, we're offering you within $2,600 of what you paid for your car." And he wrote $2,600. "That was well over four years ago. When you figure it out, Mr. Ziglar, that only cost you about $600 a year to drive that beautiful Oldsmobile." Then he lowered his voice and with a twinkle in his eye he said, "And Mr. Ziglar, you can't drive a Chevrolet that cheap."

Sales Point #17: If the customer isn't buying, you may need to do more selling.

Sales point number 17: If the customer isn't buying, you might need to do more selling. Now what was Chuck selling with that point about the Chevy? He was selling doubt. I thought to myself, *Ziglar, you clever rascal. While* *other people pay $600 a year or more to drive a lower priced vehicle, here you are driving this magnificent, great big old Regency Oldsmobile for just $600 a year. Man, I really like that.*

Then all of a sudden it hit me as to what Chuck was doing and I took that pad away from him and said, "Now, wait a minute, Chuck, just wait a minute. I have offered you $7,000 to swap cars and that's it. That's all I'll give." Chuck didn't giggle. He didn't smile. He didn't gloat or make any type of move. He just simply stood there. And what he said—this is sales point number 18—is so important—don't panic.

Sales Point #18: Don't panic.

Had Chuck tried to sell me on that $7,000 figure when I started to crawfish, what I would have done is very simple. I would have at that point, asked for a much lower price. Now I'm coming back saying, "When I offered that $7,000 to you, that's it." Chuck, didn't say or indicate, "Got you!"

Sales Point #19: Control your emotions.

Sales point number 19 is to control your emotions. You need to be a poker player at this point. Then Chuck said very quietly, "Mr. Ziglar, now this is out of my hands. I've gone as far as I can. I'll have to go back and talk to the appraiser."

Notice now how he moves to my side of the table as he says, "But I just want you to know that I really would love to have you as a customer. So let me assure you that I'll do everything I can to get your car at your price."

Notice, *"Your* car at *your* price."

Sales Point #20: Sincerely root for the customer.

Sales point number 20: Get on the customer's side of the table. Sincerity.

Sales Point #21: Assumptive close.

Sales point number 21 is how Chuck used a very subtle version of the assumptive close. He was talking about *my* car at *my* price—talking as if he is on my side. He put me in the driver's seat. He put me behind the wheel.

Sales Point #22: Clearly state the transaction details in writing.

Sales point number 22 now takes place as Chuck begins to tie down the details. He said, "Let me go talk to the appraiser. But before I talk to him, Mr. Ziglar, let me make absolutely certain that you and I are communicating and that I understand exactly what you are saying." And he turned to a new page on his pad. "As I understand it, you will make the transaction provided the $7,000 includes all taxes, all charges of all kinds."

"Chuck, you got it right. That's exactly it."

Then he went back to see the appraiser. He was only gone a couple of minutes, and when he returned he said, "This is embarrassing, but the appraiser had an emergency and had to go home. And I just wonder, Mr. Ziglar, are you going to be able to sleep tonight not knowing whether or not you're going to own this magnificent new Cadillac today?"

I grinned and said, "Well, Chuck, I think maybe I'll be able to struggle through."

Sales Point #23: Tie down the sale.

Notice sales point number 23, as Chuck ties down the sale. He said, "Now before you go, Mr. Ziglar, let me say this. In the automobile business, we actually don't even consider it a legitimate offer unless a deposit is made. But one thing I pride myself on for over twenty years in being in the automobile business, is my ability to judge men of character. And if I'm reading you right, when you say to me that if the $7,000 includes all charges, that you're a man of your word, that your word is your bond, and that tomorrow morning, if I can get you that kind of an agreement, we're in business."

He was essentially asking, "Are you a man of integrity, Mr. Ziglar?" Do you think for one moment, I'm going to say, "No, Chuck, I'm a liar"? Uh-uh, nope. So again, I modestly admitted, "Well, yeah that's right, Chuck. If I give you my word on something, friend, you can absolutely count on it. My word is my bond." I drove away.

The next morning when I walked in my office, the telephone was ringing. Chuck was on the other end and he was so excited and so enthused, saying, "Mr. Ziglar,

I have some wonderful news for you! I've talked to the appraiser. We really worked together, and we're going to be able to swap with you for just $7,200."

I knew at that precise instant I had bought the car at my price because you can absolutely, as we'd say down home, put this in your little pipe and smoke it. When people compromise one time, whether it's on a price or a principle, the second compromise is just around the corner.

I said, "Chuck, yesterday, I was very much impressed with the fact that you gave me credit for being a man of my word. Yesterday, I gave you my word. I'd swap with you for $7,000."

"Mr. Ziglar, are you saying that is all you will give?"

"Chuck, we're not eyeballing, but we are communicating."

"I'll call you back in five minutes," he said.

About 45 seconds later, the telephone rang. "Mr. Ziglar, do you want me to bring this car to you or will you come get it?"

I kind of laughed and said, "Well, Chuck, I've always loved having my cars brought to me."

"I'll see you in just a few minutes."

Sales Point #24: Keep in touch with your prospects.

Sales point number 24: You have to keep in touch with your prospects. Chuck called me regularly after that initial purchase, especially the first few weeks. That's when your new customers—those who bought what you've sold them, almost regardless of what it is—are at their most enthusiastic best. They're excited. That's the time to get new prospects from them.

And the truth is, you will never survive in the sales world over a period of years, until and unless you can get your customers to help you sell more merchandise. Otherwise, you will burn out. You will wear out.

Sales point #25: Follow-through service.

Sales point number 25: Service after the sale. When I drove in for the Cadillac's first service call, the first person I saw was Chuck. He greeted me warmly, "Mr. Ziglar, it's a delight to see you. Let me go with you to the service department. I personally want to introduce you to the service manager and I personally want to make absolutely certain that every need you have is absolutely taken care of."

Chuck understood through our phone conversations and this personal act, that service to his customer is extremely important. You see it is true, you can have everything in life you want if you help enough other people get what they want.

CHAPTER 2

THE HEART OF YOUR SALES CAREER

I firmly believe that one of the most very important aspects of the heart of your sales career is honesty.

The Forum Corporation of Boston, Massachusetts, released a study that revealed out of 341 salespeople, 173 were outstandingly successful, 168 were moderately successful.[1] They came from eleven different companies, five different industries. They sold everything from real estate and insurance to industrial supplies, and the like.

In this study they discovered that, incidentally, all had sold for at least five years—eliminating the rookie factor. All of them had the same basic experience. Each knew how to get prospects. Each knew how to get appointments; each knew how to make presentations, demonstrating features and benefits. Each knew how to handle objections and close sales.

And yet one group was dramatically more successful than the other group.

The basic reason for the difference may surprise you—honesty. The more successful group had the trust of their customers. What they discovered is that people don't buy based on what you tell them. They don't buy based on what you show them. They *do* buy based on what you tell them and show them—if they believe. And they will only believe good people, those who are honest and sincere.

Honesty and Kindness = Sales

The second discovery about the outstanding salespeople was that they were just as kind, thoughtful, and considerate to the file clerks and administrative assistants as they are to the managers and vice presidents. They realized that all members of the home office are important parts of every sale. The sale is not complete until their product has been delivered, installed, serviced, paid for, and the customer satisfied. Until then, it really isn't sold.

When these super salespeople called in, they were just as nice to whoever answered the phone as they were to the corporate executives. They all were working together. So, yes, the very heart of your sales career starts with honesty and integrity.

When I'm away from home for speaking engagements, something that disturbs me maybe more than anything else is when the media asks me, "Mr. Ziglar, is it really true that you could sell anybody anything?" That's an insane insinuation. Only a con artist can sell anybody anything. Real professionals can only sell what they truly believe will benefit the prospect, more than the money they receive will benefit themselves.

A HEALTHY EGO

The second important aspect of the heart of your sales career has to do with ego. Herbert M. Greenberg, a New Jersey psychologist, and David Mayer evaluated almost 200,000 people over a period of seven years. They concluded that:

> "Based on the insights we gained about the basic characteristics necessary for a salesperson to sell successfully, our basic theory is that a good salesperson must have at least two basic qualities: empathy and ego drive."

Mayer and Greenberg declare that empathy is vital to the process of obtaining honest, accurate customer feedback. Once provided with a strong sense of the customer's feelings, the empathetic salesperson can react accordingly. With the use of his or her ego-driven techniques, the agent can alter the pace of discussion and weigh alternatives and options before making whatever creative adjustments are necessary to close the sale.

On the other hand, the authors assert that ego drive—a subtle need to conquer—pushes a salesperson to make the deal or else. It becomes a mission, a mandate.

Mayer and Greenberg conclude, it is an active blend of empathy and ego drive—each reinforcing the other—that will best serve the interests of a salesperson's career.[2]

SYMPATHY VERSUS EMPATHY

There's a lot of difference between sympathy and empathy. Sympathy simply means that you feel like the other person feels. Empathy means that you understand how they feel, but you don't feel that way. Because you don't feel that way but you do understand how they feel, you can back away from the problem and offer the solution. I want to emphasize that sympathy loses sales, and empathy creates sales.

Let me give you an example. Many years ago I was the number one cookware salesman in the United States. I was working with the Salad Master corporation in Dallas, Texas, and living in Columbia, South Carolina. I was selling cookware to everybody in sight.

One day, I was visiting with an associate who also represented the company but we weren't in the same part of the organization. He was starving to death as a salesman. As we sat and talked at his home, he was singing the blues.

I said, "Well, Bill, I know what your problem is."

"Man," he said, "tell me quick. I have to make some sales!"

"The problem is simple. You don't believe in what you're selling."

Bill about blew a gasket. "What are you talking about? I left the company I'd been with over five years as a manager to come with this company as a salesperson because the product is so much better."

"Bill, pedal that baloney to somebody else." And with that, I nodded toward the stove in his kitchen.

"Oh, you mean the fact that I cook with our competitor's set of cookware?"

"Exactly."

"Oh, Ziggy," he said, "don't let that enter your mind. Nothing could be further from the truth. I believe we have the greatest set of cookware on the American market. But, Zig, I've had some difficulties. My wife's been in the hospital for two weeks, and I can't work when I'm worried.

"And after I wrecked my car I had to borrow transportation for six weeks. And I couldn't sell when I had to depend on a taxi and the bus and borrowed cars and all. Now it looks like we're going to have to put the boys in the hospital to get their tonsils out. And I don't even have any insurance."

I said, "Bill, how long have you been with this company?"

"Five years."

I asked, "What was your problem last year? And the year before that? And the year before that and the year before that and the year before that? Bill, let me tell you exactly what happens. When you're in a closing situation and you get down in the short rows and you ask the obligating question...I can see it now.

"The prospect looks at you and says, 'Oh, I don't know Bill. Doggone it all. We sure do need to buy a good set of pots, but now's not the right time. Bill, my wife's been in the hospital a couple of weeks and I can't work when I'm worried about her. Our car was wrecked not too long ago and for six weeks we had to depend on borrowed transportation, so I couldn't work much. And now the boys may have to have to be in the hospital to have their tonsils out and we don't even have any insurance.'

"Bill, prospects will bring up the excuses just like you've been doing for years. You can tell yourself you're a positive thinker, but deep in your mind you're thinking, *I don't know how to sell this stuff.*

"Bill, if you don't hear me say another thing, hear me when I say that selling is a transference of feeling. If I can make you feel about the product I'm selling like I feel about the product I'm selling, you *will* buy my product."

I continued, "Bill, you *must* own and use a set of the cookware you're selling. If you have to mortgage your furniture, do it."

"You really think it's that important?" he asked.

"I *know* it's that important."

Well, to bring the story to a close, I sold him a set of the cookware.

Now, obviously he wrote his own order. But the interesting thing is that Bill made enough extra sales that week to completely pay for that set of cookware. Now, why was that? Very simple. He knew he had sacrificed. He knew he had to dig deep to make the purchase. And then when prospects started giving excuses, Bill could honestly, sincerely, and conscientiously say, "Yes, indeed. It's fully worth whatever the price is. It'll make a difference in your home."

Sympathy loses sales—
empathy wins sales.

For a long time *sympathy* had been losing sales for Bill. Now *empathy* was making him sales.

Another example. A good friend of mine was president of a company that sold smoke and fire detectors and water for purification. He told me about working one evening with a new young salesman who was rehearsing a sales presentation. When he finished the pitch and then asked the obligating question, the president rocked back on the two hind legs of the chair and folded his arms across his chest.

Then he told the young man about a prospect who had told him all about a car accident and hospital bills and going from two incomes to one and a son who wrecked his car and smashed a $7,000 sign and he didn't have any insurance and his mother-in-law was in a very expensive nursing home and she didn't have any insurance either.

The president told the new salesman, "That's a whole lot of trouble. If you have sympathy for the guy and say, 'Oh, that's too bad. You're really going through a lot! Won't the government help you? How about the Red Cross? Will some of your neighbors help you? Maybe the church can do something?' that's sympathy and will lose the sale."

"Rather," my friend told the young man, "you should have *empathy,*" meaning that he understood how the prospect felt, but could back away from the problems and look at the solution like a pro.

He continued the story. "I looked right at the prospect and said, 'Tell me, in addition to all that, is there any other reason why you can't go ahead and install this equipment in your home?' The guy laughingly said, "'No, those are all my problems.'"

Then the president told the young salesman, "I simply reached down into my sample case, picked up a smoke detector, moved over to the wall and showed the prospect exactly how it would look. Then I said, 'Sir, from what you tell me, you now owe nearly $30,000. Three hundred dollars more won't make any difference at all.'

"But the thing that got me the sale was when I said, 'Sir, fire under any circumstances is devastating—but in your case, it would wipe you out.'"

This was a significant sales lesson for the young salesman—and for you. The president had taken all the reasons, all the excuses that the prospect had given him for why he couldn't buy, and used them as reasons why he *must* buy. Almost without exception, you can take the reason people give you for *not* buying and use it as the reason why they *should* buy.

A POSITIVE ATTITUDE

The third important aspect of the heart of your sales career is your attitude. I say it over and over, "Business is never either good or bad 'out there.' Business is either good or bad right between your own two ears."

In the little town of Victoria, Texas, there was an insurance salesman who always went the extra mile, understanding that you can have everything in life you want if you help enough other people get what they want. For a number of years, once a year, he asked speakers from all across the United States, paid them their full fees, and invited all of his clients to come in for an evening of inspiration. His clients sat down front but others from the community were also welcomed. It was a marvelous way to create a tremendous amount of goodwill.

During the recession in 1982, I called this guy and asked, "How is your business doing during this downtime?"

"Well, you know, Zig, there's a recession going on in the minds of some people—but I decided not to join. Actually we do 98 to 95 percent as much insurance business today as we did last year."

He continued, "But the average insurance salesperson figures that during the recession, people are not in a buying mood—so about half of them don't really work. Here's the way I figure it, Zig. I figure that if half the competition were gone and we had 95 percent as much business still available, surely I could at least double my business during the year."

Interestingly enough, that's exactly what he did! Positive thinking, your attitude is so important. What is positive thinking and what is positive believing?

Positive thinking, according to my definition, *is an optimistic hope.* I've seen positive thinkers move some mountains. I've also seen them get their teeth kicked in on occasion, including in the sales world. But I'd rather be a positive thinker than a negative thinker—and I'd rather have a positive thinker than a negative thinker on my team.

But what is a positive believer? *Positive believers have that same optimistic hope, but with reasons for believing they can move mountains.*

Positive believers sell more than positive thinkers.

Contrary to what many people think—things are not anywhere close to being equal in the sales world. The opportunities are equal, but the salesperson who goes out to sell and doesn't know how to prospect, how to get appointments, how to make a good presentation, how to close, or how to handle objections—in other words, the one who hasn't acquired any professional skills—that salesperson doesn't have the same opportunity for success as other salespeople.

Training is a significant key. Positive believing means you've utilized and taken advantage of available training, books, tapes, seminars, sessions, and training programs your company has to offer that make a huge difference in your success. Yes, it's true that positive believers will sell more than positive thinkers. Believe in yourself and your skills.

THREE RESERVES

The next important aspect of the heart of your sales career is your reserve. There are three-plus-one kinds of reserve: physical reserve; mental reserve; spiritual reserve; and love. Let's look at each one individually.

Physical reserve

Selling requires a lot of energy. I'm one of those guys who happens to believe that our physical condition is extraordinarily important. The average salesperson works about eight hours a day. The first seven hours of the day they spend working for everybody else. They make their house payment with what they earn, their car payment, or they take care of the insurance and the food and clothing, and all of the other things. The last hour that salesperson ought to be working for themselves. The problem is, by the end of the day too many of them, as we used to say down home, are too pooped to pop. I mean, they have run out of energy. You need to build physical reserve.

There are some basics to consider when you aim to be in good physical condition:

- Take care of your body by eating the proper diet.

- Get a reasonable amount of sleep every night.

- Get involved in an exercise program.

- Stop putting poison in your body—alcohol, cigarette smoke, drugs, etc.

When you take care of your physical body, you will be dramatically surprised at the difference in your sales results. Years ago I put myself on a diet and exercise program and it dramatically increased my energy level. I work considerably longer hours today than I could when I was 25 years old. Build a physical reserve and you build a mental reserve.

Mental reserve

One thing I can never understand is salespersons who do not listen to audiobooks.[3] When you're in your car, by all means on your way to calls or on your way to your office on your way to work, you should be listening to motivating and encouraging audiobooks. On your way home, or if you work from your car between calls, you need to be listening to people who offer wisdom and humor and ways to improve your sales.

I believe the most important time to listen to audiobooks is first thing in the morning. Choose successful people who inspire you and listen to what they have to say. When you start the day with an inspirational recording, listening on your way to that first call, it makes a beneficial difference in your attitude and the way you are received by the prospect. Build your mental reserve.

Spiritual reserve

You need to build a spiritual reserve, which is the foundation of your being, of who you are. I learned something astonishing, and yet it really wasn't. It was just so delightful to learn that everybody believes in God. Now that might surprise you just a little bit when I say that, but yes, everybody does believe in God.

I was talking with the chairman of the board of a major trucking business that had, at the time, more than 300 terminals and offices throughout the United States. I was surprised to learn that every new employee was required to take a lie detector test. One of the questions asked of the thousands of employees over the years: "Do you believe there is a God?" In every case when the employee answered "No," the needle on the polygraph jumped off the chart, meaning the person lied. Build a spiritual reserve—it will make a positive difference in every aspect of your life.

Love

And the final reserve type we're going to examine in the world of selling to build your career, the very heart of it is love. This probably surprises you. By now you know that selling can be a tough career, maybe the toughest thing you've ever done. But in the world of selling the toughest thing I believe is the most important thing—love.

You may be shocked to read about love as part of a sales career, so I'm going to tell you a story about it.

I love to play golf. Everyone who knows me knows I love to get out there and hit that little white ball around the course. There's nothing I enjoy more than teeing up that dude and rearing back and really driving it down the fairway.

Boom. Hmmm, I don't know if I can find it.

So I hit another one...and again.

When first playing golf, I discovered that a fast game and a slow game both require about five hours, hours away from home. So one day I came up with an absolutely brilliant idea, I bought my wife and my son a set of golf clubs. Everybody was really excited about it—except my wife and my son.

Over a month or so, they went along with me for about five games. At the end of the fifth game, the redhead (my wife's pet name) said, "Honey, I just don't like to play golf. It's too hot or it's too cold or it's too wet or it's too dry or too something. It's just not my game, count me out."

There went golf buddy number one. At the end of the summer, my boy said to me, "Dad, I don't hardly know how to tell you this because I know how much you like to play golf. And I know you like to be with me, Dad, and I like to be with you too. But, Dad, golf is just not my game. I'll play football with you. I'll go to the games with you. I'll play catch with you. I'll go fishing with you. But golf is just not my game, Dad."

Well for the next three years, there wasn't much golf in my life. Then one night I was back in Dallas in the middle of the week and we three went out to eat. On the way home we passed the Dowel Rich driving range and all of a sudden, my boy said, "Dad, let's stop and hit a few." Well, my sticks were in the trunk of the car, so we stopped to hit a few. We were soon banging away, and after a couple of minutes, he said, "Dad, let me borrow one of your woods."

I handed my son the four wood. He choked up on it a little bit, he swung back, and then let string out! I mean he busted that little dude right down the middle, about 40 yards farther than he'd ever hit a golf ball before in his life. When he turned around, I knew I had myself my golfing buddy. Second most beautiful smile I've ever seen on that face.

Now the *most* beautiful smile was two days later. We were out at the club playing, we were on one of the par fours.

He took that four wood again, choked up, and let the string out. He poleaxed that dude right down the middle. Had a little draw on it, hit the ground running like a scared rabbit, stopped dead center, right in the middle of the fairway. Perfect position.

When we got to the ball, he took his five iron out and just like you see golfers do it on television, he kept his head down and smooth stroked that ball. It took off and when it was right over the green, it landed just as soft as a feather, about 40 feet from the pin, he's hunting his bird. (That means if he sinks the putt, he is one under par on this hole. If that doesn't mean anything to you, it simply means he "done good.")

I showed the boy how to line the putt. I showed him how to stroke the ball. And when he stroked that putt, the instant he stroked it, there never was any doubt about it, it was in the cup all the way.

When that ball hit the bottom of the cup, that boy of mine jumped straight up about six feet. Still beat me to the ground by five seconds. You talk about excited! Wow, was I excited! He was excited! I grabbed him and we hugged there for about two minutes.

Then all of a sudden it dawned on me. I had a problem. You see, I was on the green in two also. I was hunting my bird too. I was only about 10 feet from the cup. I knew if I missed it, my son would figure I had done it on purpose, which would have given him a cheap victory. So I determined I was going to do the very best I could so that if I did miss, I could honestly say to my son, "Congratulations, son, you've won it. Fair and square."

I lined the putt as carefully as I've ever lined a putt in my life. My best effort always includes a little providential help. Now I don't know what you think about that, but personally, I think it's perfectly legitimate. Even on a golf course, maybe especially on a golf course. Anyhow, after I lined the putt, I stroked the putt and just like it had eyes, it went straight to the bottom of the cup.

Before I reached down to pick it up, I looked at my son and said, "Now son, tell me the truth. Were you pulling for Dad? I think you know what it would have meant had I missed."

He was 11 years old at the time. He had never beaten his dad at a hole of golf. It would have meant a tremendous amount. Yet quietly without any hesitation and very firmly my son looked me right in the eye and said, "Dad, I always pull for you."

Now you see, *that's* what we need more of in Dallas, Portland, Buffalo, and Washington. It's what we need in every home in every county, in every state in this great land of ours. It's what we need between parent and child, husband and wife, teacher and student.

Surprisingly enough, maybe it's what we need between the salesperson and the prospect. Yes, it is. Because when you are selling and they are weighing their decision, your belief in what you're selling and the benefits it will give them should be so strong that you are pulling for them to buy for their benefit.

If you can honestly and sincerely do that, then your career will catapult upward because it is absolutely true. As a wise man said, "People don't care how much you know until they know how much you care."[4] You can persuade through your heart, the right procedures, the right techniques, the right words, and the right voice inflection, which can make a major difference in closing every sale.

As we conclude this chapter about the heart of your sales career, you'll notice we talked about honesty, ego, attitude, reserve, and toughness. Taking the first letter of each of these words forms an acrostic for HEART. And the truth is, when you add love to your heart, you will sell your way to the top.

NOTES

1. Harvey Mackay, "How to Adopt a Sales Mindset," *Entrepreneur,* November 7, 2011; https://www .entrepreneur.com/article/220658; accessed May 18, 2021.

2. David Mayer and Herbert M. Greenberg, "What Makes a Good Salesman," *Harvard Business Review Classics,* 1964, published in *Royal Examiner* article, "Empathy + Ego = Sales," *Royal Examiner.com,* January

18, 2019; https://royalexaminer.com/empathy-ego
-sales/; accessed May 18, 2021.

3. Today you have many options for listening to
   motivational and inspirational speeches, blogs,
   ebooks, mp3 downloads, vlogs, podcasts, etc. on your
   phone, laptop, tablet, and computer.

4. This quote has been attributed to many people,
   including President Theodore Roosevelt, John
   Maxwell, Earl Nightingale, and others.

CHAPTER 3

FOURTEEN REAL-LIFE SALES LESSONS

In 1968, we moved to Dallas, Texas. I was conducting sales training and motivational classes from nine o'clock in the morning until nine o'clock in the evening, six days a week. Now, that's about as busy as a person can get. There were five of us living in a motel room— me, the redhead and three of our four children. It was so crowded, so my wife, Jean, the redhead, and I talked at great length about buying a house. We finally decided on what was a reasonable price.

I know the price was reasonable because she explained to me that it was reasonable. To me it seemed like the foreign aid bill to the world, but she assured me everything was all right. So she started searching for a house. And to give her full credit, she really looked at two houses. When she walked in the front door of the second one, the search ended. She found what she was looking for as our home.

You need to understand our discussion about that house. We had agreed on a certain price, and then all of a sudden she said to me, "Honey, suppose we found the dream home. I mean, exactly what we're looking for that will end our house hunting for all time. How much more can we invest than the original amount we talked about?"

Well, we wrestled with that one over and over, and we finally arrived at a figure that was an additional $20,000. Now, I know what you're thinking, *In today's market, $20,000? What are you? The last of the big-time spenders?* But let me explain. In 1968 in Dallas, Texas, after people had bought a lot, they could literally buy quality housing for around $10 or $11 a square foot.

So when I'm talking about an additional $20,000, I'm talking about a *bunch* of extras. Today for another $20,000, you can maybe get a nice little carport or a small patio, but in those days it was a whole lot more. So that's what she went out looking for and that second house had it all.

I remember it as if it were yesterday, I walked in the motel room that evening a little after nine o'clock when I'd finished the session, and she was seated on the king-size bed. She was so excited that the bed was vibrating. She hopped up and ran over to me and said, "Honey, I found the house! It's absolutely magnificent, in a real nice section of town, it has four nice bedrooms on a great, big lot, with a huge garage."

"Well, sweetheart, how much does the house cost?"

"Awww, honey," she said, "you're going to have to see it. Every single bedroom has a walk-in closet. It has four baths, and the backyard is plenty big enough for you to build that arrow-shaped swimming pool you've been talking about. And the bedroom, the master bedroom is so big we're going to have to get a riding vacuum cleaner! Honey, it is absolutely magnificent."

"Sweetheart, how much does that house cost?"

She finally told me that it was $18,000 more than the maximum, which we had already agreed, at least in my mind, was $20,000 more than we had any business at all to spend or to invest. I bellowed, "Sweetheart, we can't invest that much money in a house!"

"Well, I know that, sweetheart. We really don't know anything about real estate values here in Dallas. So I asked the builder to stop by tomorrow evening when you finish your class and take us all out at the same time to see the house. That way you can kind of get a feel for the market."

"Well, I'll go look at it," I said, "but I just want you to know in advance, that's all we're going to do. So we can kind of get a benchmark to go from."

"Well, don't worry about it," she said.

My wife, Jean the redhead, had learned a lot about selling during the years we had been married. And she was using this circumstance to reveal what an excellent student she was while "auditing" my at-home classes. Her technique was infallible.

SALES LESSON #1

Sales lesson number one is simply: when possible, *establish value before you give the price.* That's very important. Now, if you'll notice, Jean told me about the bedrooms and the walk-in closets. She told me all about the huge master bedroom. She told me where I could build a swimming pool. She told me about the neighborhood. She told me a lot of things about the "product." She was establishing value before giving me the price.

SALES LESSON #2

Sales lesson number two: *always establish value before you ask for the order.* If you don't establish value before you ask for the order, you come across as a high-pressure salesperson who wants to make the sale quickly so you can get out of there and see somebody else or get rid of this prospect so you can see someone else. No, don't do that. First establish value, then ask for the order.

SALES LESSON #3

Sales lesson number three is to *get the prospect involved with the product as quickly as possible.* The redhead said the builder would come by the next evening and he would take us to look at the house. Well, when we pulled up in the driveway of the house, I knew I had a problem. It was absolutely exactly what I was looking for—beautiful neighborhood, wonderful ranch-type home, and at that point I did something that your prospects have been doing to you all of your life, and that brings us to sales lesson number four.

SALES LESSON #4

Please remember that *your best prospects are the toughest ones to get the appointment with.* Why did I resist going to see this gorgeous house? I knew from what she had said, it sounded exactly like what I wanted. And I didn't want to see that house at that point because I was afraid of something that brings us to lesson number five in the world of selling.

SALES LESSON #5

When we walked into that house, I acted as if I had no interest at all. You see, the lesson is this, *your best prospects often show no interest.*

Why in the world would I indicate to that redhead I had no interest in the house? Why would I display no interest? The reason is very, very simple. I was afraid that if I showed any enthusiasm at all in that house, the redhead and the builder would gang up on me and talk me into doing something I already wanted to do, knew I had no business doing, and was scared I was going to do if I gave them any encouragement at all. And that is buy a house I did not, honestly at that moment, feel that we could afford to invest in.

When we walked into the house, an interesting thing happened. There was a nice entrance way with a neat little chandelier, and although my redhead never had dramatic training—I know she hasn't. I don't think so—as we walked in, she looked over her shoulder at me ever so slightly, paused a second, glanced up at the beautiful chandelier, and walked on. Message delivered, message received.

SALES LESSON #6

When she walked into the den, she immediately started *giving me ownership of the whole house.* As we toured the home, she said, "Honey, look what a big, beautiful den this is; and look, honey, this gorgeous fireplace. And notice all of the bookshelves where you can put all of your books. And over here, honey, we're going to place the television set, and I can see you now with our big, oversized sofa over here. This den has plenty of room. I can see you laying on that sofa on Sunday afternoon, watching the

Cowboys out of one eye and watching the fire burn in the fireplace with the other eye." Then she said, "Look back here!" And she led me down the hallway.

We walked into the master bedroom and she said, "See what I told you, honey? There's plenty of room here. We can put the king-size bed over here, and you know how we like to have coffee in the morning together. Well, we can set up a little table over here and our chairs here, there's plenty of room, honey. And just look at your closet. I mean, even as messy as you are there's plenty of room for all your clothes in your closet. And look here, honey."

She opened the back door and walked out. "You see what the backyard looks like? I've measured it off. We can put one end of the pool up here and we can put the other end of the pool right down here. And then we'll go right into the big garage. Look, honey, plenty of room here for your two cars. And if you'll notice here is a place 11 by 11 where we can build that little office you've been talking about."

Yeah, she was really giving me ownership all the way through. And that is sales lesson number six, right there.

SALES LESSON #7

And then finally, when the house tour was all over, she reached over, squeezed my hand and looked up into my eyes, all five feet of her and said, "Honey, how do you feel

about this home?" Now that sales lesson number seven—
*ask the prospects how they **feel**, not what they **think**.*

Interestingly enough, people buy emotionally. They
buy with their heart, not with their head. How did I feel?
I said, "Well, sweetheart, it's beautiful." What else could I
say? I mean, there I was. You think I'm going to look down
at that smiling face looking up into my eyes and say, "No, I
don't like this house. It's just a wild idea you got. No way."
I couldn't do that.

So I said, "Sweetheart, it's absolutely gorgeous. I would
love to have it. But we cannot invest in a home this
expensive."

And she said, "Well, you know I knew that honey, but I
just wanted you to see a house that was really nice. Now,
we'll go look at something cheap."

Now, come on. You don't think she was trying to shame
me into doing anything, do you? She's not that kind of a
girl. Well, nothing else was said that night. And actually,
that is sales lesson number eight.

SALES LESSON #8

Sometimes you need to back away. Sometimes you need
to let the prospect breathe when you have the luxury of
doing so. When would that be in this occasion? Obviously
we were going to be together the next morning or if you
have a ride back to the office or something of that nature

and your prospect is still with you. Let the person breathe and collect their thoughts. Sometimes they need to let the facts soak, and they're mulling in their minds as to whether or not, or how could they handle this particular situation?

Well, the next morning I was in the bathroom brushing my teeth, and I know you'll agree that when you have a mouthful of toothbrush and paste, you're handicapped as far as speech is concerned. Just then my redhead walked in and asked, "Honey, how long do you think we're going to live in Dallas?"

"A hundred years."

She asked again, "Really, how long?"

"A hundred years. I love Dallas. I hate to move. This is centrally located. This is where I want to stay."

"No, really, I want to know how long you think we're going to live here?"

Again I said, "From here on end. I love this city."

"So you really think we'll be here thirty years?"

"Absolutely, we'll be here thirty years. Why do you ask?"

She said, "Honey, I was just thinking that $18,000…"

She forgot all about the $20,000. I say she forgot. I wonder, did she? She forgot about interest and taxes and insurance and all of those other things.

She said, "That $18,000 spread over thirty years. Now, how much would that be a year?"

"Well, that would be $600 a year."

She said, "How much would that be a month?"

"Well, $600 a year, that's about $50 a month."

Then she said, "Well, how much will that be a day?"

"Now, sweetheart, come on. You're math is just as good as mine is. That would come out to about $1.70 a day. Why are you asking me all of these questions?"

SALES LESSON #9

And she said, "Well, I was just wondering if you would be willing to invest another $1.70 a day to have a happy wife instead of just a wife." Guess where we lived for the next seventeen years? That's right. In the beautiful house in the nice neighborhood in Dallas, Texas.

Now, I want to establish something very important. My wife did not let the *why* be a stumbling block but focused on the *how* we could buy it. Sales lesson number nine out of this story is this: *even though I'm "knowledgeable" about sales training and sales technique, really good technique in the hands of a really motivated person is extremely effective.*

SALES LESSON #10

Sales lesson number 10 is that my redhead did what you need to do. She *made the product affordable.* How could I honestly say I could not come up with another $1.70 cents a day? Now, obviously I know it would be more than $1.70 a day, but what the professional salesperson always does is *make it easier for the prospect to buy.* That is exactly what she was doing.

SALES LESSON #11

Sales lesson number 11 is to know how to *ask a lot of questions.*

SALES LESSON #12

Sales lesson number 12 is to understand what your sales objective is when you make a sales call.

You may be thinking, Well, that's crazy. Everybody knows that. The objective of a sales call is to make a sale. Oh, everybody does understand that, but what kind of a sale? What price sale? You clearly understood what Jean's objective was—to make an $18,000 sale. The house cost more than that, but was her objective was to sell me on the $18,000.

You see, before we ever left the house, she had already sold me the original price. She'd already sold the additional

$20,000 that the house was going to cost. Now all she needed to do was complete the $18,000 sale.

Now that fact is extraordinarily important for this reason. Let's say, for example, that you're in the automobile business and a couple comes in and say to you, "Look, our payments cannot exceed more than $400 a month if we're going to be able to trade with you."

You find exactly what they need and exactly what they want, but the payments come through at $475 a month. Now, you have a $75 a month sale in front of you. They had bought the $400 before you even entered the picture. You had nothing to do with that. Their needs and wants had already established the $400, just like in real estate.

If, for example, a couple said to you, "Look, $250,000, that's it. That's max. That's as far we can go. Here's what we want for it." They detail exactly what they want for $250,000. You find exactly what they want, but the price is $280,000. You don't have to make a $280,000 sale, you have to make a $30,000 sale.

Now, why is that so important? It's important because psychologically, and from your perspective, it's easier to sell the additional $30,000 than it is the total $280,000.

SALES LESSON #13

Sales lesson number 13: you need to *know as much as possible about your prospect.* In my homebuying example, obviously since we had been married for many, many years, Jean knew a lot about me. You will never get that well acquainted with all of your prospects. You can't work on somebody for years to make a sale and expect to survive in the world of selling unless you're selling some powerfully expensive products. So what am I getting at? My redhead knew the one thing I very much wanted in life.

When I was a youngster in Yazoo City, Mississippi, I was invited by a buddy of mine to go swimming at the country club. It was a hot day that summer, so I rode my bicycle to the club. I was wearing my bathing suit and was ready to hop in, but my buddy never showed. There wasn't another person around and the water looked so cool and inviting that I couldn't resist. So, into the pool I went. I knew I had no business doing that because unless you're a member or with a member of the club, others were not allowed to swim.

Consequently, I was in the pool no more than two minutes when a club member who traded at the store where I worked, came by playing golf and saw me swimming. He knew I had no business in the club swimming pool and told me to come see him the next day.

To this day, I vividly remember that visit in his office. It was one of the toughest things I've ever done. I thought that fellow was going to be awfully hard on me. I was literally afraid I was going to be put in jail. Even though I was scared to go see him, I was more afraid not to go. When I left his office, with tears in my eyes and my own childish anger and frustration, I said, "One of these days, I'm going to build me a swimming pool bigger than the one at the country club in Yazoo City, Mississippi!"

I'm here to tell you that in the summer of 1969, we built a swimming pool that was one foot longer than the one at that country club, back all of those years ago. Very important: know as much as possible about your prospect. My wife capitalized on knowing me well when she showed me where everything was, especially the large backyard.

SALES LESSON #14

Sales lesson number 14: *don't miss the sale because you don't have what the prospect asked for.* Sometimes a prospect asks for a product that isn't available. And think about this too—a lot of people don't really know what they want because they don't know what *is* available.

When we moved from Columbia, South Carolina, to Dallas, Texas, I said, "Now, sweetheart, because you will be spending most of your time at home with the children, you should be the one who makes the selection, but there are three things I do want: a home with a swimming pool; an office space where I can write; and the third is a circle driveway."

Well, this home she chose had an awful lot of extras, but there were three things it did not have. Any idea what those three were? That's right. No swimming pool, no office, and no circle drive. Yet the redhead used that as a sales plus, saying, "Look honey, you can design your own pool. Here's where you can put your office. You can design your own circle drive." I wanted that house, and we bought it for a lot of different reasons, but there are five basic reasons why prospects won't buy from you.

FIVE REASONS PEOPLE DON'T BUY

The first reason people won't buy is because in their minds, they don't need what you're selling. I want to emphasize that salespeople are not necessary to sell *needs*. You need salespeople to sell *wants*. I ask you, how many television sets do you *need*? How many suits or dresses do you *need*? How many groceries do you *need*? When wants go beyond need, that's when salespeople come in handy.

When wants go beyond need, that's when salespeople come in handy.

The second reason people don't buy is because they don't have money to make the purchase. Now it is true that some people don't have the money, but I don't want to mislead you along these lines. And I certainly, for those of you who are new in the world of selling, don't want to discourage you; but on the issue of money, some people will lie to you. Let me tell you a fact. Most people in corporations buy what they really want. Not necessarily what they need, but what they want.

The third reason people don't buy is because they're in no hurry. I so well remember, as a young salesman, I read this poem and committed it to memory about not being in a hurry:

> *The bride white of hair is stooped over her cane.*
> *Her footsteps, uncertain, need guiding.*
> *While at the opposite end of the church aisle*
> *with a wide toothless smile,*
> *the bridegroom in a wheelchair comes riding.*

Who is this elderly couple? Two people who waited to marry until they thought they could afford it.

The role of the professional salesperson is to impart a sense of urgency in the mind of the prospect because there's seldom a perfect time to buy anything—you can't wait until all the lights are green before you travel downtown. If you can impart to the prospect the importance of starting and handling this phase to begin with, then yes, they can go ahead and enjoy ownership.

The fourth reason people don't buy is because they don't want what you're selling. Oh, that reason is so tough for us salespeople to understand. How could anybody not want this great product, as good as it is? Oh, they don't want it, though. Now that's where our opportunity comes in as salespeople.

The fifth reason people don't buy is because they don't trust you. Very few people will come out and say, "You're lying to me. That product won't do all of those good things. It's impossible. You're lying about it and exaggerating." You will miss more sales and never know why because you have communicated along the way to the prospect something they just didn't feel quite right about buying. And you'll never know why.

The most important part of the sales process is the salesperson.

That's why I say over and over that the most important part of the sales process is the salesperson. You can't be one kind of *person* and another kind of *salesperson*. Prospects won't buy the product unless they first buy you—your honesty, attitude, and sincerity.

CHAPTER 4

WORD PLAY

I do not exaggerate with this statement—every salesperson in the world of selling today must have a way to record their presentation. Hearing yourself give your sales presentation will make a substantial difference in your productivity.

I suggest that when legally possible:

- Record the way you make an appointment.

- Record your entire presentation.

- Record the way you handle objections.

- Record your closing.

- Record everything you say related to the process of selling.

When you have recorded and listened to the recordings, you will discover that what you actually say and what you tell your sales manager you've been saying are two entirely different things.

I suggest that after you listen to the recordings, write it all down. You're going to be absolutely astonished at some of what you discover.

REMARKABLE DISCOVERIES

First, you will probably discover that you talk entirely too much. That almost always shocks salespeople who record what they say and then transcribe it word for word.

The second thing you discover is that you often hear what the prospect says, but really miss the essence of what the prospect is *really* saying. You will notice that too often you give non-answers to objections and miss a lot of closing opportunities.

Listening intently to the recordings, you will discover that you and/or the prospect may often go off on tangents, which are absolutely incredible. And during long interviews, you might discover your voice becomes monotone as your enthusiasm wanes, which really does make a difference in effectiveness.

You may be thinking, *Well now wait a minute, Ziglar. The way I sound on a recording and the way I really sound is not exactly the same.* Oh, I've got news for you, it really is the same. The reason it sounds different from when you listen to yourself talking is because the sound is literally coming through bone. Now I'm not calling you a bonehead, I'm just saying the sound of your voice comes through bone.

ONE SENTENCE BUT EIGHT DIFFERENT MEANINGS

When you record what you say, it comes back through the air and that's the difference. I suggest you record, first of all, one sentence: "I did not say he stole the money." Those are eight simple words, yet that sentence can say eight entirely different things.

Record the sentence until your closest friend, spouse, or your salespeople can clearly identify all eight things you're saying.

First of all, "I did not say he stole the money" is simply a statement of fact. But by changing the inflection of your voice, you can indicate eight different meanings with the same words:

- "I did not say he stole the money!" Totally different meaning with the emphasis on "not."

- "I did not say he stole the money." Not him, the rascal with the money right is over there.

- "I did not say he stole the money." Someone else may have implied he did, but I didn't.

- "I did not say he stole the money." He was just borrowing it and would return it.

- "I did not say he stole the money." The rascal took her jewels, not the money.

- "I did not say he stole the money." I may have suggested it but I didn't say it.

- "I did not say he stole the money." The rascal may have stolen money but not this money.

You see what I'm saying—the *way* you say what you say makes a huge difference in what the person hears you saying.

Prospects will give you their price objections in a variety of ways. Sometimes a prospect says, "That price is ridiculous!" That's a pretty strong reaction, isn't it? Others may say, "Well, the price is a little high." Even though the objections and tones of voice are different, you have to handle them in exactly the same way by repeating the objection.

To the one who said, "That price is ridiculous!" you lower your voice, look the person right in the eye, and simply say, "The price is ridiculous?" That tactic sounds so simple, but I can guarantee you, it works. It's a very simple way to move the objection back to the prospect's side of the table. Now the prospect has to defend the statement versus you justifying the price. And there's a dramatic difference in the overall results.

Once in a while a prospect may look at you and say, "Well, it seems to me that price is a little high." It might be a low-ticket item, so you might simply respond,

"Well, let me ask you, Mr. or Mrs. Prospect, just every once in a while, don't you think you deserve something that is just a little high?" What you're really conveying to the prospect is, "It's amazing what something like that will do. Why not treat yourself once in a while? You deserve it."

One of the most effective and most powerful closes I know is when you simply lower your voice as you look at the prospect and say, "Well, you know, Mr. or Mrs. Prospect, many years ago, our company decided that it would be easier to explain price one time than to apologize for quality every time. And I'll bet you're glad we made that decision. Aren't you?"

OVERCOMING OBJECTIONS

Does that sort of thing work in the real world? Yes. An insurance representative in Tucson, Arizona, said to me one day, "You know, Zig, one night I was on my way to my biggest sales opportunity. The proposal I had, if the prospect bought, was worth twice as many dollars in business as any contract I'd ever written. But I was really dragging bottom that night, so I listened to a recording of yours on the way to the meeting. I'm so glad I did because you talked about repeating objections to the prospect. And sure enough, when I got down to the close after I'd made the proposal, the prospect just kind of dogmatically said, 'Well, that price is too high.'"

The man continued, "So I almost verbatim did what you said to do in that situation, but with a little twist at the end. I looked the prospect right in the eye and said, 'Mr. Prospect, many years ago the founders of this company made a very important decision, they decided it would be easier to explain the price one time than to apologize for lack of service on claims and benefits forever. And deep down, Mr. Prospect, I have an idea that you're delighted they made that decision.' The prospect was awfully quiet for a few seconds, then said, 'You're right. I'll take it!'"

The right words, right intentions, right voice inflection, and right concept will make an absolute major, positive difference in selling your way to the top.

Sometimes, after you've answered one objection, two objections, three objections, four objections, it might be that the prospect will then say, "Well, it doesn't make any difference what I bring up, you've got an answer for everything."

Now at that particular point you are either close to making the sale or close to missing it. What you say next and the way you say it will make the difference. After a compliment like that, if you modestly admit you were number one in the region for the past two months, then you have just fed your ego. And nothing else is going to happen.

But if you want to make the sale, you will get out of the way and let your product and your persuasive ability take over to benefit the prospect. So, you lower your voice, look the person right the eye and say, "Well I really appreciate that comment. And I'm going to take it as a sincere compliment, but the truth is, there are many questions I don't have the answer for. That's one of the reasons I'm so excited about selling this product, which is the answer to your needs. And that's really what you want, isn't it?"

I'll say again, with the right product, right words, proper inflection, and most importantly, the right intent—you are a successful, professional salesperson.

Now, I'd like to share an example of how this can be put together in an effective presentation.

About ten years ago, I was passing through St. Louis, Missouri, and had a little time to invest. I was drawn toward the carousel, close to a shoeshine stand. I needed a shine so I walked up to the small room and noticed that all four of the guys were busy shining shoes. There were no empty chairs so I stood at the entranceway. In a couple of minutes the young man in the third chair finished shining and his prospect put his newspaper down as he climbed out of the chair. The young man pointed at me and said, "You're next."

I climbed up in the chair and sat down. While young shoe shiner finished the cash transaction with his customer, I was looking at the prices. A regular shine was 75 cents, the wag shine was $1, and the spit shine was $2.

I thought, *I'll get the 75-cent shine, tip the guy a quarter, and I'll be on my way.* According to the young man's name tag, Johnny came over, sat down on the seat facing me, looked up at me and asked, "What kind?"

I said, "I'll take the regular."

He literally stood up and took a step backward, looked at me again and asked, "Regular?"

I should've known then that I was in for an unusual shoe shine. But I wasn't about to let that dude get the best of me. So I said, "Yeah, you guys do such a fantastic job, and I'll be on my way in a matter of minutes."

There was no response, he didn't even grunt. Johnny just sat down again and reached over, got his saddle soap, and quickly put it all over both shoes. Then he used a drying cloth to dry my left shoe and then the right. As soon as he finished, he ran his fingers over the leather and the squeak was probably heard from a block off. The shoes were squeaky clean.

He said, "Man, these are really nice shoes."

"Well, thank you very much."

He said, "They're Ballards aren't they?"

"As a matter of fact, they are."

He said, "Don't they cost a lot of money?"

"Oh brother, do they ever! But I do a lot of work on my feet so I really need comfortable shoes."

He said, "I bet they're comfortable, aren't they?"

"They are very comfortable."

He had, by then, finished drying the shoes off and he reached over to get the polish to put on them. But before he did, he reached up and grabbed my pantleg and said, "Man, that is the most unusual piece of cloth I think I have ever felt."

"Well, it actually is an unusual piece of cloth. My good friend in Fort Madison, Iowa, who sells me my clothes, told me that this piece of cloth comes from Ireland. He guarantees it's going to last me at least five years. And I believe it will because I've already been wearing it a couple of years, and I can't even tell that it's not a brand-new suit."

He said, "What kind of suit is it?"

"It's a Hickey Freeman."

"Man, those dudes do cost money."

"Yeah, they're not inexpensive, but the cloth on this one made it especially expensive. But I'm convinced I have a real good buy."

That suit lasted nearly ten years. I had the lapels altered so it was in style and after about eight years I had a new lining put in it, but other than that, it remained a beautiful suit. While I was sharing with Johnny all that suit history, he was shining away. I don't know how much you know about shoe shining, but when you hear that cloth popping, it has nothing whatever to do with the shining. That's merchandising, that's sales talk. I'm in favor of that, all the way.

Johnny was trying to attract the crowd from outside to come in and see what was going on. He was shining and popping like the expert he was. Then all of a sudden, between pops, he stopped, backed away, looked right into my eyes and said, "You know, it just seems like a shame. Man will spend over a hundred dollars on a pair of shoes. He would spend several hundred dollars on a suit of clothes. And all he's trying to do is look his best. Then he won't spend another dollar to get the best-looking shoe shine in the whole world to top off all of the rest of it."

I said, "Spit on them, man. Spit on them."

I don't know about you, but when I get a 75-cent shine, a quarter tip is all right. But whoever heard of a quarter tip on a $2 shine? I mean, folks with class just don't do things like that. So, I took a dollar to go with the two and I handed it to him. Man, I strutted out of there with a smile on my face—talk about a high stepper!

Old Zig was picking them up and putting them down, thinking to myself, *What in the world is this guy doing shining shoes?* Then I looked up at the clock tower and it showed exactly ten o'clock. It clicked as I looked. And that's important because when I sat down in the shoe shine chair, it had clicked three minutes before the hour.

I was in his chair three minutes. I gave him $3. Now you do not have to be a Phi Beta Kappa from MIT to figure that one out. That would be 60 bucks an hour or $480 a day. While writing this in the 1960s, a psychiatrist makes $60 an hour!

I know what you're thinking, *Yeah but Ziglar, me and you both know that he doesn't make $480 a day.* I know that. Cut it in half, make it $240. Cut that in half, make it $120. Cut that in half, make it $60. Sixty dollars a day figures out to be more than $18,000 a year.

But tan a dog in Georgia, I guarantee you if that dude ain't making over $30,000 a year shining shoes. He's good. He's real good. But let's not get confused here. The reason he's doing that is, number one, he is a professional salesperson. One of the best I have ever seen. He goes out after business. When things are slack at his stand, he goes out about a hundred feet away and starts bringing people in. He delivers what he sells. When he sells that shoeshine, he delivers every bit of it.

You know, I personally believe our rate of divorce will decline about 95 percent if we delivered in marriage what we sell in courtship. I believe our sales careers would catapult forward if we would deliver everything that we sell. Keep our promises.

I want to emphasize that Johnny was a professional. He's the only shoe shiner I have ever seen who wore a name tag. Not only did he have his name on the tag, he had his title: Shoe-ologist.

There's an interesting sequel to the story.

I was back in the same area a couple of years later, and I walked by the stand and looked in. No was there except Johnny. I walked in, hung up my bag, and Johnny said, "Have a seat."

When I sat down, I noticed the prices had changed. Regular shine was $1. And "spit shine" was changed to the "best shine."

After I sat down Johnny asked, "What kind?" Well, I didn't want to go through that again. So I said, "Give me the best." I found out a long time ago that people work better with praise than any other way. So I told Johnny my appreciation of him as a professional.

He acknowledged the compliments. And since no one else was there, he just kept shining. He put polish on and shined, put it on again, and shined again. I finally had to say, "Well, Johnny, I have to go." So he finished, did a beautiful job. As I stepped down, he said, "You know, you've been asking me a lot of questions. Do you mind if I ask you a couple of questions?"

"No, go right ahead."

He said, "I can't help but notice that you have an overnight bag. Does that mean you're going to spend the night in St. Louis?"

"Yes. I am."

He said, "Do you by any chance have another pair of shoes in that bag?"

"Well, as a matter of fact, I do."

He said, "You know, it'd really be a shame to have the best-looking shoe shine in St. Louis tonight and look like one of the guys tomorrow. It won't take me but a minute, you'll be on your way."

That time I left $5 with that dude.

But here's are my two questions for you: Do you think I was upset when he wanted to shine my other pair of shoes? Or do you believe I was delighted that he had asked for the business in the way that indicated he wanted me to look good to the public?

There are significant lessons we can learn from this story.

Number one, Johnny honestly believes he is the best shoe shiner on the face of this earth. You don't believe it? Just ask him, he'll say, "None better than me, man. Nobody is better."

The second lesson he can teach us is the fact that he believes in his product. His own shoes were shined to a standstill. He was representative of what he was selling. When I looked at his shoes, I, and others no doubt, said, *That's the way I want my shoes to look!*

Number three, a lesson we sales professionals can learn, is that he was a hard worker. When business slacks, as indicated earlier, he goes after it; but when he is shining, he is really working diligently on each shoe.

Number four, he's enthusiastic. Everyone loves to be around enthusiastic people.

Number five, he's adaptable. My first exposure to Johnny was when he was shining a guy's shoes who was sitting there reading the newspaper, obviously interested only in reading his paper. Johnny said nothing to him. He let the guy do what he wanted to do. He let him read his paper. He talked to me because it was obvious I wanted to talk.

Lesson number six is that Johnny asked the prospect to buy. Now I tell you, that is significant.

And the seventh lesson, he didn't hesitate to upgrade and add to what the prospect was already buying. The truth is, it's a very simple matter. Most of us are calling on customers whom we've dealt with in the past, who are currently buying from us. We have additional products to sell, and yet for whatever reason—fear of being considered pushy or whatever, or the fear we might lose the business we already have—we are not offering the additional services we have.

Now, don't misunderstand that. I don't believe every salesperson should offer every prospect or every customer, everything they sell, every time. But I do believe, on a regular basis, you should offer an additional product that you're excited about—one you know your customer is buying from someone else. Give them the opportunity to consolidate their orders with you.

It's not a question of you selling them something they neither want nor need. You are offering them something they're already buying—maybe of a lesser quality at a higher price—from someone else.

Yes, you are servicing the accounts. You are doing what the professional really ought to be doing. Yes, the professional is truly a well-balanced person. Someone who looks at all phases of selling. That is a given.

Like Johnny, a professional has integrity, is knowledgeable, and is aggressively caring in a creative approach to solving the problems of the prospect. Whether that is a needed shoeshine, cosmetic dentistry, dependable transportation, a computerized program, or an investment approach to life that makes sense.

The professional salesperson provides what is needed with integrity and persistence and with the customer's best interest at heart. That's how you sell your way to the top.

CHAPTER 5

SIX KEYS TO SALES

Now we're going to look at six important keys to selling your way to the top. We are going to discuss these important keys in reverse order—saving the most important for last.

KEY #6—LISTEN

Number six is listen. Listening is key to selling successfully. It's hard, if not impossible, to listen your way out of a sale. As a matter of fact, on everybody's list of desirable qualities, a good listener rates right up there at the top.

You have probably by now learned how to listen, but there are a few aspects that I really want to emphasize. For example, when a prospect says no, we oftentimes don't hear it—because we don't *want* to hear it.

We also need to learn how to listen not just with our ears, but also with our eyes. When the prospect says to you, "No, I wouldn't give you that much money" while he is stroking the upholstery of a nice new car, his mouth may be saying, "Too much money and I won't buy it," but his body is saying, "Look friend, all you have to do is convince me. I'm interested. Make it worth the money to me and I'll go ahead and buy."

Or another prospect might say, "Nah, that's too far out of town," and then the couple walks to the back bedroom and look out that big picture window at the gorgeous view. You need to always listen not only with your ears, but also with your eyes.

And as mentioned before, there are instances when we really don't want to listen—as when someone says no. I have a good friend, a most remarkable lady. She had one of the most peculiar hearing problems. A customer could get right down in her face and say, "No. I don't want to buy." She wouldn't bat an eyelash. She hadn't heard a thing. (Yet I've seen someone whisper yes at 60 paces and she picked up absolutely every syllable of it.)

Subjective listening is critical.

This friend was one of the most consistent people I've ever seen in the world of selling. She was professional. She had memorized how to handle objections. She had memorized her closes to the degree that they were so natural, no one would ever even remotely suspect they were memorized.

I watched her sales calls a number of times and she always used the same process and the same phrase that worked. She would make it her business to be seated directly in front of the prospect, usually a woman, but as she started her closing, she would invariably pick up her chair and move it to beside the prospect, then she would reach up and put her hand on the lady's shoulder. Next, she always said exactly the same thing, "This is so beautiful and you deserve to have it, and I'm going to hep you get it." That's right, she said, "I'm going to hep you get it." Not help, hep.

Watching, hearing, and listening to her tell the prospect she was going to help her get that cookware, it seemed as if the two of them were going to gang up on that big old cookware company. She made it seem as if they could conspire together—the company has thousands of sets of cookware, and bless your heart, you, Mrs. Prospect, don't even have one, and I'm going to hep you get it.

When she moved her chair closer to the prospect, she was not only physically closer but also closer emotionally and every other way too—she moved to the prospect's side of the table in more ways than one. Learn to listen; but when the prospects say no, please understand that the reason they say no is because they don't "know" enough to say yes. They don't know enough of the benefits. This key is a most important key.

KEY #5—PERSISTENCE

The next key is the most misunderstood key. It is the key of persistence. Many people think of a persistent salesperson as someone who sits on you until you give in. "You're going to get it sooner or later, sign here. Oh you know you want it, all your neighbors are getting it. Sign here." That's not persistence, that is downright foolishness. Those are the kind of salespeople who are not exactly a credit to our profession.

I really didn't understand what real persistence was until a number of years ago when I was touring Australia with World Book Encyclopedias. I was working with the managing director, and we were speaking in all of the major cities in Australia for World Book. During the trips, the director and I did a lot of chatting. He shared with me a story, which has had a substantial impact on my career, and it happened to have a tremendous impact on his career as well.

John started as a part-time salesperson, as many of us did when we first entered the world of selling. He was on a sales call one evening, calling on a German couple who had been in Australia about six months. Their command of the English language was very, very limited. The woman had given birth to their one and only son when she was 44 years old.

John started the sales presentation at eight o'clock in the evening. It was after midnight before the sale was closed. When John left the couple's home, the lady went with him through the front yard to the fence gate, as they had a vicious dog and she had to escort him.

After they walked outside the gate and closed it, the lady reached up and put her hand on John's shoulder and said, "Thank you. Thank you, young man, for staying till we know what these books will do for our boy. Thank you. Thank you."

John said it gave him a completely new understanding of the importance of what he was doing.

If you believe in what you're selling, you will persist.

You see, I believe there's a better word for persistence—belief. I believe that if you believe in what you're selling, you will persist. When you believe, you will sell professionally, politely, and as courteously and graciously as you can.

The professional will persist if he or she fervently believes that the prospect benefits with ownership of what you're selling. It certainly gave me a new perspective on the word after talking with John and hearing this story.

KEY #4—IMPENDING EVENT

The next key is the impending event, which is anything that happens in your industry or to your company or product that has an impact or an influence on your prospects and customers.

For example, if your company is going to introduce a new product line or service, you will want to sell your clients on the concept that something new and exciting is coming their way. You want to prepare them for the "impending event" that will benefit them.

When I was in the life insurance business, when an individual is six months and one day past the last birthday, the person is now considered a year older in many statistical tables, and we used that as an "impending event." Consequently, we capitalized on that with this emphasis, "Mr. or Mrs. Prospect, if you buy today, if you invest today, then the truth is you will save this amount of money." That specific impending event really made a significant sales opportunity. We need to be tuned in to all of our products' particulars if we're going to sell as much as we should be selling.

KEY #3—INDUCEMENT

The next key is kind of unusual—the key of inducement. Inducement is another word for enticement or incentive. A story that begins with my cuff links tells it all. I have a set of cuff links that I just happen to believe are the most beautiful cuff links in the whole world. I really do. My dear red-headed wife gave me the cuff links for our 25th wedding anniversary. Of course they're in the shape of an arrow. An arrow pointing up is our emblem—see you at the top!

When I received the cuff links, I made myself a promise. I'm not going to wear any shirt again unless it has French cuffs so I can wear the cuff links. So I went shopping for French cuff shirts. This was a number of years ago. I walked into several stores and asked, "Do you have any French cuff shirts?" The response, "No." I went into a dozen different stores. "You got any French cuff shirts?"

"No, I don't."

"Do you know where I can get them?"

"No, I don't. Besides that, don't you see I'm busy? I was talking to this other clerk here." Now that wasn't exactly what was said, but it was almost that bad.

Not long after, I was speaking in Burlington, Iowa, for the Chamber of Commerce. While there I noticed a gentleman wearing a white suit. I thought, *That's the sharpest looking suit I've ever seen. Self, you have to go get a suit just like that.* So I cornered the fellow and asked him where he got it. He said, "I bought it over in Fort Madison at Glasgow Clothiers."

"Well, I think I'm going to scoot over there tomorrow morning and get one just like it."

He said, "I'm actually going over tomorrow morning. I'll be pleased to take you along."

"That'd be wonderful."

We arrived at the store and he introduced me to Doyle, the salesclerk.

"Doyle, do you have a white suit?" I asked.

He asked, "What size do you wear?"

"I wear a 41."

He said, "Yeah, I have that size."

He brought out the suit and I slipped it on, perfect fit. He measured the trousers to cuff them.

"When will the suit be ready for me to pick up?"

He said, "Well, I thought you said you weren't leaving until 2:00."

"That's right."

He said, "Well mister, you're going to take this suit of clothes with you." And then he turned to a young man standing close by and said, "Take this suit of clothes upstairs to the tailor. Tell him I want it right now."

Then Doyle turned to me and smiled and said, "Now Zig, I have something I really want to show you."

I left that store with two suits, three sport outfits, five pairs of slacks, and all of the good stuff that goes along with it. As we were concluding, something was said about shoes.

"No, Doyle, I'm well pleased with my shoes. I don't really need any." He didn't hear a thing I said.

"Man," he said, "you have to look at these," and right straight to the shoe department he went. As it turned out, I didn't find any shoes that I really liked that day. But as I was getting ready to leave, and as an afterthought, it truly was, I said, "Oh, by the way, Doyle, do you have any French cuff shirts?"

He said, "No, I don't. But I can get them."

A couple of weeks later, I received a telephone call from Doyle. I had ordered a half dozen shirts from him so I could see the quality and how they looked, all that sort of thing. He was calling to find out if I received the shirts and if I liked them. I did.

About a month later, I called him.

He said, "Zig, I was just going to call you."

"Yeah, and I know what you're going to tell me."

He said, "You do?"

"Sure. You're going to tell me that you just received a new shipment of the most beautiful suits you have ever seen in your life. You're going to tell the company that you will be sending a dozen of the suits to me so I can pick out exactly what I want, and then I'll send the rest back."

He said, "Zig, you are a genius."

There's a chance that Doyle is saving me money. He declares on his Scout's honor that he is, and he might well be. But let me tell you what Doyle is really saving me—*time*. I spend less than an hour a year choosing my clothes because he sends me the clothes that he thinks I will like, based on our longstanding relationship. I take what I've selected to the tailor not far from our house and close to my barbershop where I go frequently. This relationship is a most unusual one but mutually beneficial.

Now I don't even bother to ask about the price, and he never tells me the price because over the years we have developed a relationship based on absolute trust and integrity. He simply sends me the clothes; if I like them, I keep them and pay for them. If I don't like them, I send them back.

Now why am I devoting such a tremendous amount of time on this one simple example of inducement? Because it is full of good advice. Neither of us know the exact dollar amount he made over the years, but I've an idea that Doyle's business has reaped at least a half million dollars, maybe as much as a million dollars considering the number of years.

Now obviously I haven't bought that much clothing. But just as obviously, from telling this story in my book, presentations, audio presentations, and seminars, Doyle tells me as a result of all of this conversation, people call him every day and say, "Hey, if you treat me like you treat old Zig, we're going to do some business together."

There's no such thing as a little sale.

What's my major point? There's no such thing as a little sale. There are sales that grow. You know the story. From a small acorn grows the mighty oak. And from a little sale, a lot of times you build a tremendous amount of business.

What's the inducement? I believe the greatest inducement of all is the personal interest and integrity of the salesperson who believes that by serving the needs and meeting the needs of prospects, he or she is going to benefit as a result. It's part of my overall sales concept—you can have everything in life you want if you help enough other people get what they want.

KEY #2—SINCERITY

The next key is what I believe to be the most import-ant key—sincerity. So many salespeople have told me that they made the sale because the prospect felt they were sincere. The prospects have said, "I turned down three other people. But I'm giving you the business because you seem so sincere in what you're saying."

See, selling is a transference of feeling. When you can make your prospect feel about your product like you feel about your product, if it's humanly possible, they're going to end up buying your product. Selling is the transference of feeling.

You have to sincerely believe in what you're selling.

Now don't hang your hat too much on just being sin-cere. You have to sincerely believe in what you're selling; and if you're sincerely interested in your prospect's best interest, you will want to learn as much as you can, as a professional, to use the right procedures and the right techniques to help them purchase a product that will benefit them.

KEY #1—POSITIVE PROJECTION

The following story, or event, is an effective way to help you remember the keys shared in this chapter about successful selling. A number of years ago on a Saturday morning in Columbia, South Carolina, I walked into the den and said to my son who was four years old, "Son, would you like to go to the grocery store?"

He said, "Sure, Daddy." And he hopped up from the floor and put on his little boots. We jumped into the car and drove to the grocery store. As we walked into the store, I picked up a basket and turned to the right to start gathering food. My son had seen a display of rubber balls straight ahead and made a beeline for the balls. He grabbed a ball out of the display and ran over to the basket, and he plopped that ball right into the basket, then stood there grinning from ear to ear.

At that point I had never talked with my son at any length about this, but I have an idea that when I said to him that morning in the den, "Son, would you like to go to the grocery store with Dad?" the reason he said, "Sure, Dad," in that little active four-year-old mind, he was already thinking, *If I go with my daddy to the store, I'm going to get something. I don't know what it is, but I'm going to get me something*. He was already using the key of positive projection.

The instant we walked in, he assumed he should make his move, which he did with a considerable amount of enthusiasm. That boy used four "keys" on me in about four seconds flat.

When I saw what he did, I reached into the basket, took the ball out, and said, "Son, you already have a dozen balls at home. You don't need another one." And I handed it to him. "Now take it back."

My boy looked up at me and said, "Daddy, can I just hold the ball?"

Well, what would you have done? I mean the boy is only four years old. He doesn't want to buy the ball, he only asked me a very simple, subordinate question. What kind of daddy would I have been if I said, "No, boy, you can't even hold a ball. Now take it back." I wasn't about to do that. So I said, "Okay, son. You can hold it a few minutes, but don't get any ideas. You are not going to buy that ball." He didn't want to buy it, he just wanted to hold it.

We walked around a few minutes and when we passed by the display of rubber balls, I reached into my son's arms, took the ball, and put it back in the display, saying, "Son, you've held it long enough. You might fool around, drop it, get it dirty, and then Dad will have to buy it. You don't need another ball." With that, I turned and walked away.

Well, my boy was not listening when I said no, because he went right back to the display, snatched that ball right back out, ran to the basket, plopped it right back in, and again, stood there grinning at me. I have to confess that he was one persistent little salesman.

Well, I'm kind of persistent myself, so I reached into the basket, took out the ball, and as I headed for the display said, "Son, I've told you for the last time now, you cannot have this ball."

When I started to walk back to the display, I looked down and there he stood, all 39 pounds of him. At that time he talked with a slight lisp, and he looked up at me and said, "Daddy, wish you buy me that ball, I'll give you a tiss." That was an impending event, I'll tell you. You talk about an inducement! What else could a four-year-old boy give his daddy? In my lifetime I have never dealt with a more sincere salesperson ever before or since.

Now I'm going to tell you this, I don't think it's necessary, but I will anyhow. For a long time thereafter in the Ziglar household, we had *13* rubber balls.

I had said at times that I've never seen where a woman had given birth to a salesperson. But that's not quite true because in Columbia, South Carolina, the local paper carried a small headline and the following announcement: "Birth of a Salesman Announced. Mr. and Mrs. Zig Ziglar announced the birth of a salesman, John Thomas Ziglar born February the first, 9:04 PM Providence Hospital, Columbia, South Carolina." Now don't misunderstand,

I'm not trying to influence my boy's career. I mean, he can sell anything he wants to. That's up to him.

And if you buy these ideas and use these keys, you too can sell more of what you're selling and you will have a more successful career as you sell your way to the top.

CHAPTER 6

MIND'S-EYE SELLING

"How do you want me to introduce you for the program? Do you want me to introduce you as a speaker?" I've been asked this question many times over the years, and I always say, "No. Please tell them I am a teacher." I believe that a *speaker* informs, often inspires, and entertains people. But a *teacher* gives the audience information, advice, stories they can take home and use that day, that week, that month, that year, and year after year. What they hear from a teacher has a big and different impact in people's lives.

The words we use can make a dramatic difference in how we "see." I became aware of this several years ago when I was in Indianapolis, Indiana, having a meal at an upscale hotel. When I looked at the menu, I thought to myself, *Oh wow, this menu was written by a salesperson who really knows how to use words to paint a picture and entice an appetite.*

The following were some of the dishes:

- Spanish Supreme, a tumultuous arrangement of fresh spinach leaves mingled with enoki mushrooms. (Let me stop right here. Do you know what enoki mushrooms are? Tell me the truth. But don't they sound good?)

- Crisp chips of bacon and ripe tomato with our superb hot, bacon dressing.

- And for protein lovers: Mr. Chopped Sirloin conducts an orchestra of fresh vegetables, fruits, and eggs, to an audience of shredded lettuce with an accompaniment of frozen yogurt and cottage cheese.

Can you imagine a better use of words?

Likewise, the sales professional can take a verbal paintbrush and paint the prospects right into the picture, giving them the satisfaction and gratification of visualizing in their mind's eye the use and enjoyment of what they are selling.

The following is one of the most fascinating little incidents of life, a blurb is all it really is, and yet it says so much. Several years ago, *The New York Times* ran a story about a minister and his wife, a New Jersey couple who were selling their home. The real estate people ran the ad that was beautifully written. It was great, it was factual, and it read like this:

> Cozy six room home, ranch style with fireplace, garage, tile baths, all hot water heat, convenient to Rutgers campus, stadium, golf courses, and a primary school.

Now those are facts, but we as professional salespeople need to clearly understand that people do not buy facts. They don't even buy benefits for that matter, unless they can see those benefits translated into their own personal use. Well, that ad ran for three months and the house still had not sold.

The Mrs. decided to take matters into her own hands and with *her* verbal paintbrush the ad now read:

> We'll miss our home. We've been happy in it, but two bedrooms are not enough for us so we must move. If you like to be cozy by a fire while you admire autumn woods through wide windows, protected from the street, a shady yard in the summer, a clear view of winter sunsets, and quiet enough to hear frogs in the spring, but prefer city utilities and conveniences, you might like to buy our home. We hope so. We don't want it to be empty and alone at Christmas.

Now let's look at that ad closely for a moment, really exploring all of the pictures painted there. Incidentally, the very next day she received six calls and sold the house to one of the six callers.

Now, back it up in your own mind's eye and let's look at the pictures.

- "We'll miss our home." That picture gives you a feeling of sadness.

- "We've been happy in it." They love their home; the second picture.

- "but two bedrooms are not enough for us"— that's not negative about the house, it's just not big enough for them. It's also factual, telling the reader how much room is there.

- "so we must move." They might have stayed but the family outgrew it.

- "If you like to be cozy by a fire" and who doesn't, really?

- "while you admire autumn woods through wide windows" What a great picture of looking out wide windows and seeing all the fall colors.

- "protected from the street" You feel safe. It's secluded. It gives you and your family privacy.

- "a shady yard in the summer" Cool and enjoyable.

- "a clear view of winter sunsets" Now that's romance.

- "and quiet enough to hear frogs in the spring" I don't know what you think about frogs, but all of a sudden, I thought they were pretty nice.

- "but prefer city utilities and conveniences, you might like to buy our home. We hope so. We don't want it to be empty and alone at Christmas." You almost feel sorry for the house, don't you? I mean, you don't want that house to be alone, especially at Christmastime.

Word pictures, or what you see in your mind's eye, sell because they appeal to the heart—and people buy with the heart. Everybody is a salesperson, and everybody sells. So, selling words are extremely important.

What prospects see in their mind's eye sells, because people buy with their heart.

As we get involved in the teaching process about the use of words, some words are negative and some words are positive. My sales trainer friend Tom Norman put together a list of essential words regarding selling. Let's look, first of all, at some of the positive words.

The first positive word, of course, is the prospect's name. We all agree that's a very positive word to use frequently so the prospect knows he or she is important to you. Other positive words in this line of work:

- Understand
- Proven
- Health
- Easy
- Guarantee
- Money (Financial Resources)
- Safety
- Save
- New
- Love
- Discovery
- Right
- Results
- Truth

- Comfort

- Proud

- Profit (we business people like that one)

- Deserve

- Happy

- Trust

- Value

- Fun

- Vital

Yale University adds a few words to that list:

- You

- Security

- Advantage

- Positive

- Benefits

And two of what I consider the most beautiful words of all:

- Faith

- Hope

You should *avoid* the following negative words:

- Deal (I can't imagine any professional salesperson using the word deal)
- Cost
- Pay
- Contract
- Sign
- Try
- Worry
- Loss
- Lose
- Hurt
- Buy
- Death
- Bad
- Sell
- Sold
- Price
- Decision
- Hard
- Difficult
- Obligation

- Liable

- Fail

- Loud

- Ability

- Failure

- Pitch (one of my least favorite of all words in the sales vernacular. I can't imagine a professional using that word.)

Of course profanity is an absolute no-no. And the worst of all is saying God's name in vain.

It's important to use the right words—positive, motivating words. Eliminate negative, unmotivating words. You need to build your presentation on the positive record of the product or service using positive words.

Sometimes salespeople, you know, we get to talking, and you know, everything they say, you know, after you've been listening for, you know, a minute or two, well, you know what I say, you know, when I'm talking about this, you know, don't you?

Have you ever been listening to someone and the person has you climbing the wall in about nine seconds flat because they repeat the same phrase over and over? "You know" what I mean?

Do you understand what I'm saying? Do you? You understand what I'm saying? I mean, do you understand what I'm saying? You know what I mean? Know what I mean? You know what I mean? Do you know what I mean?

You can go bananas.

And occasionally, I've been around someone who has been told to use the prospect's name all the time. So what do they do? They use it way too often. "Well, Mr. Jones, here's the thing, Mr. Jones. Mr. Jones, if you consider this, Mr. Jones. Mr. Jones, if you watch, you'll find, Mr. Jones, that this, Mr. Jones…" and absolutely in about a couple of minutes, it's driving Mr. Jones out of his gourd. That is why we need to be aware of what we say and what words we are using. It's another excellent reason we need to regularly record our presentations and really listen to them to hear what we're actually saying.

Words can make a dramatic difference—good or bad.

When I think of salespeople, I think of one of the greatest salespeople I have ever met. He's a dentist. I'll never forget when I went to see Tom for the first time professionally. I had been hearing about him from several of our staff members who were patients. I went to see Tom to have some teeth capped, and I was really impressed with several aspects of his practice.

First of all, three people worked on me before I ever saw the dentist, and each one of the three smilingly said exactly the same thing, "Mr. Ziglar, the doctor suggests that you only floss the teeth you want to keep." Now that gentle admonition really told me something. I thought, *Here's a man who is interested in preventative dentistry and wants me to keep my teeth.* I really appreciated the way the sentence was phrased.

Any successful businessperson, medical or otherwise, who has a service or product of value has a moral obligation to sell to everyone who can afford and who needs what you have.

As I listened for positive words while in the waiting room, I noticed that the dentist's consultant mentioned "restoration" of a tooth, not a "filling." People don't want to have their teeth filled. They said, "change in schedule," not "cancellation." They called to "confirm" the appointment, not to "remind." While in the chair, I was asked to "empty my mouth," not "spit." My teeth were "prepared." I received an "injection" not a "needle" or a "shot." I did feel a little pressure but no pain.

Successful businesspeople who have a service or product of value has a moral obligation to sell to everyone who can afford it and needs it.

I really want to stress this point—every professional has a moral obligation to sell his or her service if they're good. For example, I have a close friend who went to another dentist at about the same time as I did, and this friend had been told that he had nine teeth that should be capped. Now, interestingly enough, he was fully covered with insurance, but when he looked at the bill for nine teeth he thought, *That's so much money. I'm not going to ask that insurance company to pay that.* And so he asked the dentist, "Do I really need to get all nine capped right now?" And the dentist said, "Well, no. Five need capped right now, but the other four can wait."

He prepared the five teeth and never said another word. Didn't even ask him about insurance, and didn't ask when he was going to have the other four capped. Although my friend has been back to that dentist two or three times since then, he still hasn't completed the job for the other four teeth. Now I say for several reasons, that dentist did not perform the services that he should have performed as a professional. There are several factors involved.

First of all, when my friend eventually chooses to have the four capped, the chances are the new caps will not cosmetically match the older ones. They may be close but the teeth won't be cosmetically as attractive. Number two, there will be another investment of several hours and additional pain involved. Number three, there will be some additional expense involved. And number four, and probably the most serious of all, is the fact that my friend stands a chance, now I'll admit it's slim, of something happening and a tooth could be lost, beyond repair.

EVERYONE SELLS

I believe every professional needs to have the prospect's best interest as the priority.

I never will forget when the pastor of our church asked a couple of men to visit me to see if I would teach a Sunday school class. Well, that's quite a responsibility and it was something I was not certain I was qualified to handle because it was a rather conservative church. Of course I'm conservative, but it was a very large class and I just didn't know if I was ready to tackle it. So I said to the men, "Well, I'm flattered that you asked. I really don't know. I will certainly carefully consider it. And then I will pray about what I should do."

The next day—I don't mean the next week, I don't mean the next month, I don't mean two days later—the next day, I received a letter in the mail from the pastor saying, "Thank you for agreeing to teach this class." Now *that's* an assumptive attitude. You see, all of us are in the world of selling.

One night while driving home to Knoxville, Tennessee, I got caught in a snow storm and spent the night in a Greyhound bus. Fortunately I made it home the next day, and I was tired and cold when I walked in the door. My wife said, "Honey, wait a minute, don't take off your stuff yet. I need you to go to the store for some things for the baby." Our brand-new baby was at home, only about four or five days old.

"Oh, okay," I said. So I put the clothing back on, a big topcoat and all, and our three-year-old daughter, Susie, came up to me and said, "Daddy, I want to go."

"Oh, Susie, the weather's too bad. I'll be back in just a few minutes."

"But, Daddy, I'll be so lonely," she said.

"Susie, you're not going to be lonely. Your mother's here, the maid is here, your little sisters are here."

She looked at me and said, "Yeah, Daddy, but I'll be lonely for you."

I don't think I need to tell you that she went with me to the grocery store to get whatever was needed.

Capitalize on the natural, the obvious things that are yours.

As a salesperson, you should capitalize on the natural things you have, the obvious things that are yours to work with. For example, a saleswoman in a dress shop tells a prospect she set some special dresses aside for her. She brings out a few items and ushers the woman into a dressing room, along with the dresses. While the prospect is changing, the saleswoman says something like, "Mrs. Jones, any of those dresses will make your husband ooh and aah when he sees you in it!" If that's not picture selling, I don't know what is.

You know by now that I'm a golf enthusiast. I love to hit golf balls. I've done some work with the Ping Manufacturing Company. Actually, I use a set of their clubs and think they're fantastic. If I were selling golf clubs, the line I would use from time to time for avid golfers would be, "Now this is our set of 'ooh and aah' clubs. Because when you step up to that tee and bust that ball right down the middle, you're going to hear your friends go 'ooh aah!'" Now you might think to yourself, *Are you kidding me, Ziglar?* Not in the least. Everything is selling and it's actually very natural.

PAINT THE PICTURE

I'm always so amazed at how many times I have over-heard conversations between ladies talking and one says something like, "My husband bought me a dress. I wear a size 12 and he came home with an 8. I can't believe he would do such a dumb thing." Or "My husband brought home a green sweater and he knows I look terrible in green."

Well, let me tell you something. I've been married now for well over forty years. I brought my wife dozens and dozens of gifts and I'm delighted to be able to say, I have never made a mistake. Not even once. I always get the right size. I always get the right color. I always get exactly what she was dreaming and hoping that I was going to get.

Now I'll be the very first to admit that I usually never see it again because she has taken it back and exchanged it for something that fits and is the right color.

What was the redhead actually doing by graciously accepting the initial gifts? She was giving me all the encouragement I could possibly need—to keep bringing her presents. Now *that's* selling! That's selling of the highest order.

When you use the right words to paint the right pictures that appear in a prospect's mind's eye, when you paint the person into the picture, you give hope and encouragement and motivate the person to close the sale.

Everything
is selling.

I never will forget that Friday evening the redhead met me at the airport. I'd been gone all week and when I saw her, she was dressed in one of those ooh and aah dresses. She snuggled up real close, slipped her hand into mine, looked up at me and said, "Honey, I was just thinking. You've been gone all week. I know you've been in five different cities and you're probably tired. If you would like, on the way home we can stop by the store and pick up some fish or seafood or maybe a nice steak and when we get home I can make a nice dinner.

"Tom's spending the night down the street, so it'll just be the two of us. It won't take me long to prepare, maybe an hour or two at the most, then the two of us can sit there and really enjoy the meal. But I know you don't want to get involved in washing a whole bunch of dirty, greasy pots and pans and dishes and cleaning up and all that sort of thing."

After a short pause she said, "The thought occurred to me that you would probably be far more comfortable if I were free to devote the entire evening just paying attention to you. I could do that, of course, at a really nice restaurant."

Everything is selling.
You can have everything in life
you want if you help enough
other people get what they want.

CHAPTER 7

COMMON TRAITS

Chances are excellent that you've noticed something that virtually all professionals have in common. Every one of them are tastefully and conservatively dressed. The reason is very simple: countless, and I do mean countless, psychological studies reveal that the appearance of the counselor, and that is what a professional salesperson is, has a direct bearing on whether or not the advice given is going to be followed.

The second thing professionals, whether doctors, lawyers, ministers, accountants, tax consultants, guidance counselors, architects, psychiatrists, or salespeople have in common is they ask a lot of questions. The reason is fairly obvious. The professional must identify your problem, your need, or desire; they find out what you want and what you need before they can offer the solution. They also know that if they ask you the right question, you will often come up with the solution. That way it's your idea. When it is your idea, your chances of enthusiastically following through are dramatically increased.

Selling isn't just telling, it's asking.

For the professional salesperson, the advantages are obvious, because it bears out the concept that you can have everything in life you want if you help enough other people get what they want. In this case, a solution to the problem.

The professional also directs the interview so that the prospect, or person being counseled, asks questions so the expert can give advice relevant to the prospect's needs and concerns. That's really what it's all about. In a nutshell, selling isn't just telling, it's asking.

Now obviously I'm not talking about the police inter-rogator or the prosecuting attorney approach, where they put someone on the griddle, so to speak. I'm talking about the counselor consultant, the helpful friend approach.

Let me share with you a story out of my own sales background. And as I share this story, I want you to notice the number of questions that go back and forth. I also encourage you to notice that when we reach a particular area of the questioning, this is where the salesperson self-image is so important. A lot of people—because of a fear of rejection or the fear of offending someone or they fear missing a sale if they pursue a particular point—are a little bit weak when they start to nail down some of their points.

I was selling cookware when we were living in South Carolina. I've always believed in "nest selling." By that I simply mean selling in a small area. When I was in the life insurance business, I used to sell either in one large building, or one very small town. I've always felt that if I drive long distances when I have prospects close by, I ought to wear a chauffeur's hat, because that's really what I was doing—just driving around. I started in the small town of St. Matthews, South Carolina, putting on group demonstrations at night. At that time, it was about 25 miles from my back door where I lived in Columbia.

In less than six months, I sold more than $40,000 worth of cookware in that little bitty town. And back in those days that was a powerful lot of cookware. I'll never forget one evening I had a demonstration for seven couples. The next day as I was making my calls, I sold the first five, and knocked on the door for the sixth one.

I remember it well. A booming voice came forth, "Come on in, Mr. Ziglar." I walked in and there before me stood this big fellow who had been at the demonstration the evening before with his wife. He was about six feet six or seven inches tall and weighed a lean 300-plus pounds. He was a big man. He said, "Glad to see you. Me and you both know I'm not going to buy no $400 worth of pots, but it's good to see you."

Well now let me emphasize a point. That big guy had eaten food the night before in direct proportion to his size. I had bought that food, cooked that food, and served that food. So his introduction to our interview wasn't exactly ideal as far as I was concerned. When he said that, I kind of grinned and said, "Well no, sir. I don't know it. You might, but I don't."

He said, "Well, might as well be up front and tell you. I'm glad to talk to you because I understand that's part of the deal so the hostess can get her prize, but," he said, "I'm not about to buy no $400 set of pots."

"Well, Mr. Prospect, looks like you and I have lots in common."

He said, "Oh, how's that?"

"Well, in my particular case, my wife spends our money and the neighbors take care of our business. And all I have to do is work. I don't know what your situation is as far as your wife is concerned, but I can tell you neighbors are taking care of your business."

"Oh," he said, "how's that?" Very jovial fellow.

"Well, I've already been to five of your neighbors who were at the demonstrations last evening and in every case, after they had bought their set of cookware," (I had to slip that one in.) "they would all ask me, 'What did Mr. So-and-so do?' And I'd say, 'Well, I haven't seen him yet.' Then they'd say, 'Let me know what he does.' And I finally asked one of them, 'Well, why does everybody want to know what this particular individual does?'"

And the big guy said, "They probably told you I was the biggest tightwad in the county."

"Well, now one of them did say something about you having your first dollar, but I'm not sure I understood what he meant."

He kind of laughed and said, "Me and you both know exactly what he meant."

"Yeah, I guess I did. But isn't that amazing? You were born and raised right in this little area."

He said, "Yep, never left five miles from here."

"Isn't that amazing? You were born and raised right here, and nobody here really knows anything about you."

He said, "What are you talking about?"

"Well, I thought you said you were not going to get the cookware."

"I'm not," he said.

"Isn't that amazing? You were raised around these people, but none of them know you."

He said, "Explain what you're saying."

"Well, Mr. Prospect, let me ask you a question. Last evening, were you sincere (Don't ever ask anybody if they're telling you the truth, that's an insult.) when you said that you knew your family could save at least a dollar a day cooking in our set of cookware? We made a big to-do about demonstrating the economy."

He said, "Mr. Ziglar, as big as my family is, I can save *two* dollars a day. I got four boys and they're all bigger than I am. And they all eat more than I do—and you know how much I eat. I could save two dollars."

"Well then, a dollar a day would be a very conservative estimate, wouldn't it? So if I cut that dollar half into fifty cents a day, that would be ultra conservative, wouldn't it?"

He said, "Yes, it would."

Now notice what I said, "Well, if that set of cookware would save you 50 cents a day, that means it costs you 50 cents a day not to have it, doesn't it?"

"Well," he said, "I suppose you could say that."

"No sir, what I say is not important. I'm talking about your money. So what do you say?"

"Well," he said, "I suppose I could say the same thing."

"No sir. Now we can take that word 'suppose' out, can't we?"

He said, "You're the most persistent guy I think I've ever seen."

"Well, I'm talking about your money."

He said, "Okay, we'll take it out. Yes, I could save 50 cents a day."

"That that means it costs you 50 cents a day not to have that set of cookware."

He said, "Okay, points made."

"Now, Mr. Prospect, what that really means is this: every two days your wife will take a dollar out of the family larder. And because she doesn't have this method of preparing the food and saving, shrinkage, electricity, and all of that, it means that she literally, every two days, will take a dollar out of the family treasury and tear that one dollar bill into pieces. Every two days she will do that. And it really amounts to the fact that she's throwing money away."

I continued, "Now, Mr. Prospect, from what your neighbors tell me," (Please understand that I'm smiling when I'm saying this.) "a dollar is a big deal to you. They tell me these eleven hundred acres of good fertile land under cultivation don't belong to you and the bank, they belong to you. This beautiful home doesn't belong to you and savings and loan, it belongs to you. But according to your neighbors, you sure do hate to see something happen to one of them dollars. But that's not so bad until you realize that every 40 days your wife will reach in and pull out a brand-new twenty dollar bill from the family treasury and she will literally tear it to pieces and just throw it away."

When I tore up a $20 bill in front of the man, he broke out in a cold sweat. Drops of sweat broke out on his forehead. Then I asked him, "Mr. Prospect, what'd you think when I tore up that one dollar?"

He said, "I thought you was crazy."

"What did you think when I tore up the $20 bill?"

He said, "Didn't think a thing, I *knew* you were."

"Mr. Prospect, whose money was that?"

He said, "I hope it's yours."

"It is. Yet, you hated to see me tear up my money. Didn't you?"

He said, "I sure did."

"Mr. Prospect, don't you feel even closer to the money that's your very own?"

He said, "What are you getting at?"

"Mr. Prospect, as I understand it, from what I was told last night, you've been married nearly 23 years. From what you told me today, you believe that you would save 50 cents a day by having our set of cookware, or it costs you 50 cents a day not to have it. That's $182 and 50 cents a year. Since you've been married more than 20 years, I want to switch it back to $180, because I can multiply it times 180 real easy. That means, Mr. Prospect, in 20 years you have already invested, paid is a better word for it, wasted maybe even, $3,600 not to have a set of our cookware. And now you tell me you won't invest $400 to have a set of the cookware. Mr. Prospect, that's government thinking if I have ever seen it in my life.

"But that's not so bad, because maybe you didn't know about this until now. But now you're saying to me, 'Look, Mr. Ziglar, in the next 20 years I'm going to spend another $3,600 in waste for a total of $7,200 not to have a set of the cookware. But no, I'm not going to give you $400 to own a set of the cookware.'"

Let me say again that I'm smiling while talking to him.

"Now Mr. Prospect, I hate to threaten anybody, but in your case I'm going to make an exception. I'm going to ruin your reputation in this community if you don't buy a set of my cookware. And the reason is very simple. These people, your friends, they think you are conservative, but me and you both know that any time a man will spend $7,200 not to have a set of our cookware, and won't give $400 to own a set of the cookware, he is not conservative, he's lost his common sense."

It was awfully quiet for a minute. And then he asked something that really impacted my sales career. He said, "Mr. Ziglar, if I buy, what could I tell my neighbors?"

Very significant. You see, people buy for two reasons: 1) for themselves, and 2) for other people. They might say it doesn't matter what anybody else is doing. Don't believe it, in most cases. Why would he ask that question? And why must we include some logic and facts for people to base their decisions on—simply so they can tell their friends, relatives, and neighbors why they bought it?

Yes. This man had assured everybody that he wasn't going to buy the cookware. He had told the hostess when she invited him, "I'll come eat the man's food, but I'm not going to buy no $400 set of pots." The night of the demonstration he was late arriving, and when he walked in his friends were kidding him, "Hey partner, I see you've come to buy that $400 set of pots."

He said, "I'm not going to buy no $400 set of pots. I've only come to eat the man's food." Now he's asking, "What can I tell my neighbors?" He's painted himself into a corner and needs a way out that will preserve his ego.

Many times prospects make a firm statement then think they can't walk it back. They may have told another salesman six months ago, "If I ever buy this, I'll buy it from you." Yet they have totally forgotten the guy's name after a day or so. If we can get them out of the corner with some dignity, the sale is a foregone conclusion.

I knew the sale was mine if I could help the man with his dilemma of what to tell his neighbors.

"I'm going to give you some words to use," I told him. "And if you'll do this, not only will your neighbors love you even more, they will respect you even more. I'm going to go ahead and write this up and mark it paid in full, because I know you're not going to fool around paying interest since you're a conservative individual."

And we both kind of laughed when I said that.

"And I'm going to give you the receipt written out across the top, 'Paid in full.' And I'm going to suggest that you take this and go see one of your friends. And when you walk in, just wave the slip of paper, they'll recognize it because they've got one the same color. When you walk in, be prepared. They're going to razz you like you've never been razzed before. Just stand there and grin. Let them go ahead and do it.

"And when they get through, look at them and say, 'Yes, I clearly said I wasn't going to get it. But when I made that statement, all I knew was the price. I had no idea what the benefits were. Then I realized it would be better for my family, that it would save my wife work, and would save me money. And then I realized I couldn't let my stubbornness stand in the way of doing something for my family, especially since I had the money, so I bit my tongue and went ahead and bought it.'"

I said, "Mr. Prospect, they'll love you more because it takes a big man to admit he made a premature decision. It takes an even bigger one to do something about it."

The big man sat there for fully a half minute. Then he slapped his leg, got up and said, "You're the doggonest feller I ever seen in my life." And he walked to the back bedroom. Back in the day in the rural South, they keep the checkbook in the back bedroom chest of drawers, third one from the top.

There is an interesting turn of events about that particular incident. From that moment on, that big guy became one of my best friends and biggest supporters. As a matter of fact, every time I scheduled a demonstration in that area, he would call up and ask the hostess who was coming. The hostess would give him the names; and as he reviewed the list, he'd say, "Well, he can get that one, yeah. He can sell that one. Oh, he won't have any trouble with that one. Uh-oh, I don't believe he can handle that one. I better come and go with him on that one."

He actually helped me sell an enormous amount of cookware in that community. I believe fervently to this day that, had he not seen the demonstration of that money being torn apart, he never would have been a customer.

QUESTIONS UPON QUESTIONS

Questions can be used in many different ways to help you sell your way to the top. I vividly remember a number of years ago when I was scheduled to speak in Greenville, South Carolina. I had written for a motel room reservation, but when I pulled into the parking lot and saw all of the traffic, I got a little nervous.

When I walked into the front lobby, I knew I was in trouble when I read the sign posted on the wall: "Traveling man, avoid Greenville, South Carolina, the week of October 11 through 15. This is textile week." I was told later that during that week in October there were no vacant rooms within 50 miles of Greenville, South Carolina. Nevertheless, I walked up to the desk and said, "My name is Zig Ziglar, would you mind checking my mail, please?" The lady was not impressed.

"Mr. Ziglar, do you have a reservation?" she asked.

"I certainly hope so, I wrote for it long ago."

She said, "How long ago?"

"Oh, it's been nearly three weeks."

She said, "Now wait a minute, Mr. Ziglar, we haven't had an opening here in over a year. We book them from one year to the next."

"Now, wait a minute..." and about that time a lady walked out from behind another counter.

"I'm Miss Fortune, perhaps I can clear up the confusion."

"You don't look like Miss Fortune to me. You look like good news all the way."

The lady smiled very pleasantly and said, "Mr. Ziglar, ordinarily I *am* good news. But unfortunately not for you today."

"Wait a minute, ma'am. Don't say another thing. I've got two questions I need to ask."

She kind of smiled pleasantly and said, "Okay, what are they?"

"Question number one. Do you consider yourself to be an honest woman?"

She said, "Well, of course I do."

"All right. Question number two. If the president of the United States were to walk through that door right now and come up here and say to you, 'I want a room for this evening,' now tell me the truth. Would you have a room for him?"

She grinned and said, "Now, Mr. Ziglar, you know perfectly well we'd have a room for the president of the United States."

"Ma'am, you're an honest woman. I'm an honest man. You have my word that the president of the United States is not going to come through that door. So I'll take his room."

I slept there that evening.

Now here is "the rest of the story," as Paul Harvey would say. The president of the group I was speaking for was actually the manager of that particular motel. And he had been unable to get me a reservation in his own motel. He said there were no rooms.

I used the same successful tactic on at least two other occasions.

You can use questions in a lot of ways. Since salespeople sell every day, doesn't it make sense to learn how to use questions more effectively to obtain the desired result? You should commit to memory hundreds of questions. You can use the question technique in all phases of life. When you learn to ask questions, when you learn to get people involved in the transaction, you are using some of the most important secrets in successful selling.

So I challenge you, do what has been shared throughout this book, and your sales career will move forward and upward faster—and you'll have more fun in the process.

CHAPTER 8

OVERCOMING OBJECTIONS

It might come as a surprise to you when I say this, but what we salespeople ought to get the most excited about are actually objections. Because if there were no objections to begin with, there'd be no need for salespeople. People would just go ahead and buy everything, and we would be out of the picture. One of the most important aspects of selling is dealing with those objections.

To begin with, let's understand the basic difference between a question and an objection. A question simply means the prospect is seeking information. How long will it take for delivery? What colors are available?

And on the other hand, people who raise an objection are actually looking for encouragement. They are really saying, "I have an interest in this, and I want you to give me some encouragement about the way I can end up owning what you're selling." No objections and no interest go together without any doubt.

BASIC FACTS ABOUT OBJECTIONS

A basic fact about objections is simply that objections are our friends—that's the first thing I want to make clear. They clearly say to us salespeople, "Yes, I'm interested in what you're selling."

And the next fact is, you don't have to answer all objections. For example, I bought a suit that I really didn't like for two reasons: I didn't like the price and I didn't like the fact I had to wear a belt. But my wife told me it was a nice fit and the color went well for me. She said, "Honey, I like it." All objections were overcome—I bought the suit.

Another fact is that approximately 90 percent of objections will be the same when you're out in the world of selling. If you hear the same objections time after time, what you need in many cases is a new presentation, or a more conclusive or inclusive presentation. Hearing the same objections indicate that you're not doing enough selling in the presentation itself.

The fourth point in overcoming objections is realizing there is a formula that fits in most cases, and you can adapt this formula and follow the formula in handling objections. However, we need to remember that there are many different kinds of prospects who look at a purchase in a variety of ways. For instance, there is the animal prospect, who's going to "bear it in mind." The insomniac prospect is "going to sleep on it." The musical prospect, who will "make a note of it," and the playful prospect who's just "feeling out the market." Yeah, there are a lot of different prospects.

The thing I believe we need to clearly understand is that all prospects, regardless of the kind, have two basic things in common. Number one, they want to be right. Number two, the prospect really wants to be understood.

WHEN AND WHY TO HANDLE OBJECTIONS

There are four times and opportunities to handle objections:

- The first time is before they occur.

- The second is when they occur.

- The third time is later on in the presentation.

- The fourth time is never; some objections just simply should not be given any credibility.

By far the most effective time and place to handle an objection is *before* it occurs. When the same one keeps coming up, as previously mentioned, you need to reorganize your presentation.

Many years ago, a man who invented a particular machine taught me a couple of lessons that I was really excited about. I used to demonstrate what he taught me at state fairs and on television. I sold lots of those machines. When I turned the crank, cleanly cut fresh vegetables would come tumbling out.

Objection #1

Invariably, we encountered two major objections. I'd be right in the middle of a demonstration and a member of the group would ask me, "Mr. Ziglar, if I bought that machine, could I use it like you use it?" I always looked at the person—usually a woman because at that time mostly women were making the meals at home—and smile and say, "No ma'am, there's no way you will ever be able to use this machine like I use it."

Now you might think that's a strange thing for me to say, but I did it for a couple of reasons. Number one, I was telling her the truth. I don't believe a busy wife and mother could ever learn to use that machine as I did, and I explained why. Basically, they have 101 other things to do around the home and they may use the machine two, three, or four times a week. I was using it several hours every single day. So it's not likely that they could do with it what I could do.

Now I would have answered her that far, but how many machines would I have sold if I had stopped it right there? Not many.

I wanted to sell machines, so here's how I continued the answer. "No ma'am, you could never use it like I do, because you have so many other things to do in your busy day. But let me tell you how effectively you can use it."

I continued, "The machine comes with an instruction book, and if I give you this book right now, and if you spend five minutes reading the book, I will give these very sharp knives to these three ladies." Then I pointed to three ladies who were closest to me.

"After you read the book, in five minutes time, with this machine, you can cut more food, better and faster, than all three of these ladies combined can cut the food with the knives. Although you've never used the machine and they've been using knives all of their lives, you could cut more with the machine. Not because you're an expert with the machine, but because you *have* the machine that does the job *for* you. And that's what you really want, isn't it?"

I used that also as a trial close.

"As you can see, you can use five different blades in this machine." I demonstrated one of the blades, cutting about seven or eight different types of food.

Then I'd say, "As you can see, we have used only one blade and we've cut all of this beautiful food. Now let me ask you, if the machine only had one blade, how many of you already feel that's something you really want to have in your home? Can I see your hands?" I would get my best prospects immediately right there. Then I demonstrated the other blades.

Objection #2

The second objection that would often come up when I was demonstrating, I would intentionally bring up myself. I'd say, "A lot of times people ask me, 'Mr. Ziglar, if I bought that machine, is there a chance I could cut my hand?' I always grin and I'd say, 'Yes ma'am, but we don't recommend it, but if that's really what you want to do, it's a very simple procedure. All it takes is coordination. (I went through the motions so they could all see.) You insert your finger as you turn the crank. Now get it straight, insert finger, turn crank, and when you do, the red comes out right here. Now if you don't want to cut your hand, keep it out of the machine.'"

This is how you sell on the offense. Your believability is greater if you handle the objections in the body of the presentation. Otherwise, you are apparently defending, instead of selling on the offense.

HANDLING FIVE BASIC OBJECTIONS

Regardless of the kind of prospect, if an objection occurs during the presentation, there's some basics you can follow, especially on the first objection, and it's appropriate to answer it at that point. Sometimes it's not appropriate, but if it is appropriate, answer it.

> Objections thrive
> on opposition,
> but die with agreement.

For example, you might be demonstrating tires and the prospect might say, "Well, I don't believe these tires are rugged enough for our use." Now what do you do?

- Number one, listen to the objection. Solomon, the wisest man who ever lived, put it this way, "He who answers the matter before he hears it is not wise."[1] Let the person explain the objection.

- Number two, act pleased that the objection was brought up. Objections thrive on opposition, but they die with agreement. "I'm really glad that you raised that issue." Don't use the word "objection," say "raised that issue." You truly should be, because that says the person is interested.

- Number three, change the objection to a question such as, "Your question is, as I understand it, will these tires hold up under the day-to-day pounding our city streets will give them. Is that what you're asking?" That way, you get the customer involved.

- Number four, you need to get a commitment from the person that this is the only question. "Mr. Prospect, is this the only question you have that stands between you and ownership of these tires, or is there something else?" You obviously wait for the answer.

- Number five, you use the question or objection as the reason for going ahead. "Actually, Mr. Prospect, the question you raised is the reason we do so much business in the city; fleet test after fleet test firmly established the fact that our super, reinforced, steel-belted radials, with Durabrig, are ideally suited for rugged, city street usage. As a matter of fact, that's the very reason that XYZ Company...." Then you parade your testimonials, and you close the sale at that point.

Now if prospects bring up another objection after you've completed your presentation, handle it in the same manner, but if they bring up yet another objection, you respond with a question. "Mr. Prospect, do you mind if I ask you a question," and you listen to their answer. Then the question is, "Is this the only question that stands between you and a favorable decision concerning our product, or would there be something else?"

If that's the only other question, you answer it, you assume the sale, and you attempt to close. If the prospect says, "Well, I'm also concerned about," and they start bringing other things out, then what you do is you take your talking pad, and whatever the objection is, it might be price, you write it down. It might be they don't know that much about your company. It might be the guarantee.

You write down each question on the pad, then you simply say, "Are these the only objections?" After you deal with each one at a time, then simply say, "Is that a satisfactory answer to your questions?" Then cross each one off after providing the answer. "Does that clarify the issues to your satisfaction," would be another way of putting it.

PROSPECTS WANT TO SAY YES

When each one is crossed off, subliminally, with that little bit of demonstration, you have shown the prospect that you have eliminated every reason for not owning the product. In essence you have shown the prospect that there is no obstacle for doing business.

As salespeople, we need to understand this. *The prospect wants to say yes.* I know that may surprise you, especially if you have had a half dozen nos in a row, but they really do want to say yes. One of the reasons is because no is so final.

There's something about humans that keeps us from totally terminating relationships unless it is a bad one—and even then it may be hard for some people. If you've been acting in a professional manner, they really do want to say yes. There's a second reason why they want to say yes: if they don't say yes to you and there's a need for this or a similar product, the person will have to talk to another salesperson. Many times prospects don't want to take the time and effort to do that again.

Some objections you encounter are better answered later. For instance, you may be demonstrating one feature, and are asked something entirely unrelated. It might not be appropriate to answer right at that moment; but whatever the other objection might be that you don't want to hound, you simply say, "Well, that's a very exciting feature of our product, and you are going to be delighted when I get to that point. But if you don't mind, let me continue with this aspect because we're at such a critical area that I need to tie some things together that are very relevant. I promise to get back to your question, but if I neglect to do that, please remind me of it."

Try not to forget. As a matter of fact, if you're wise, you'll scratch a little note on your talking pad so they can see you're not trying to put them off, that you really do want to answer the question or concern.

PLAN AHEAD

You need to plan ahead, which means you should memorize a lot of ways to say the same thing. The reason? As you memorize, you will come to realize there are a lot of ways to say the same thing, but there's only one way to say it best. Find out what that best way is, and stay with it.

Again, when they bring up an objection and you're right in the middle of an important aspect of your presentation or demonstration, don't answer right then, if possible. Act pleased, then get permission to delay, "If you don't mind, I'd like to answer that question in a moment, and I promise do to exactly that." Then close that down a little bit by saying, "Is that fair enough?" Then keep your promise.

An amazing thing about that little question, "Is that fair enough." Interestingly, everybody basically wants to be fair; so when you ask, "Is that fair enough?" they give you permission. To repeat myself, be sure you do exactly that.

Some objections are not meant to be answered, so just smile and ignore them; but if the question comes up again, regardless of how absurd it sounds, deal with it.

You're not in the "sales answering objection" business. You're in the sales business.

Here's another something that is important and you must understand, you're not in the "sales answering objection" business. You're in the sales business. On many occasions when I was training another salesperson, I would watch the person answer an objection and then would, in essence, say, "Well, I handled that pretty good. Go ahead, shoot another one at me. I'll take care of it too. Go ahead, challenge me." That's crazy. Answer the objections, then close.

Sometimes selling involves simple, brief analogies or it can involve just asking for the order. I'm thinking of a friend of mine from Oklahoma who managed a furniture store. Randy said that when he listened to our sales training tapes, he would translate the stories I told and use them with slight alterations to perfectly fit his own business sales.

He told me about a lady who came in to the store looking for a reclining chair. Her husband was getting it for her as a Christmas present, so she went to the store to pick it out. She brought her teenage daughter along and found exactly the chair she wanted. It was $449.95. She loved it, and she said to Randy, "I'll go home and talk to my husband."

Randy said to her, "I just remembered something I heard that you may find interesting. I have two children and my grocery bill runs about $100 a week."

"Well, there are three of us and that's about what my grocery bill runs," the lady said.

Randy said, "You know, I'd almost bet you that you never really talk to your husband about that grocery bill, you just go ahead and buy the groceries, don't you?"

"Yeah."

Randy said, "Interestingly enough, $100 a week is more than $5,000 a year, yet you never ask your husband about the $5,000. He's anxious for you to have this chair as a Christmas present. He's giving it to you. Do you really want to go home and talk to him about it?"

Randy said the lady looked over at her teenage daughter and then said, "I'll take it."

A simple, little analogy she could relate to.

ASK FOR IT

Another instance. I often make the statement that a lot of people don't get the order because they don't ask for it. Randy was sharing with me that a couple had been in the store because they were almost completely refurnishing their home. They had been married a number of years. The kids were now grown to the degree that they wouldn't destroy the furniture any longer, and so the order was significant. They chose furniture for several different rooms and when the bill was totaled, it was a substantial amount.

When Randy presented the cost to them, the lady just said, "Oh, that's a lot of money! We're going to talk about this."

Randy acted as if he had not heard a word she said. He looked at the husband and said, "Well let me ask you this question, when you get this are you going to want to haul it home yourself, or will you want me to deliver it?"

The man turned to his wife and said, "Well, what do you think?" Now remember ten seconds earlier she wanted to go home and think about it, but when the husband asked, "What do you think?" she vehemently answered, "Shucks no, he charges money to deliver that stuff. We'll just take it home ourselves."

GARY, SIDNEY, AND IVAN

Now let's look at three types of prospects.

First of all there's Gary Gullible. It's best to deal with old Gary in an open, straightforward way, telling lots of human interest stories. He's more likely to buy because he likes and trusts you than for any other reason. He responds to persuasion, but is offended with speed and pressure. Deal with him gently but confidently.

Then there's the other end of the spectrum—Sidney Skeptical. I especially want to remind you that a skeptical, antagonistic prospect wants to be right, and wants to be understood. When Sidney raises a dogmatic objection with a little anger, cynicism, or for that matter sarcasm hidden underneath it, you should respond by saying, "I'm delighted you raised that question, Mr. Prospect; and to make absolutely certain I clearly understand what you're saying, would you mind repeating it?" This approach solves a couple of things: it indicates an honest effort on your part to be fair, and it also indicates you place considerable importance on what the prospect is saying. Additionally, when he repeats his objection, chances are good he will substantially reduce the tone of that objection.

That situation has happened to me a thousand times in my sales career. Someone is dogmatic, even antagonistic, or very sarcastic in their objection, vehement. I always say, "I appreciate your position, but to make really certain I understand it, would you mind repeating it?"

147

It's astonishing how much softer the person's tone and attitude comes out the second time. You can deal with someone far more effectively.

In dealing with skeptical, antagonistic prospects it's important not to argue or contradict what they're saying, even if they're wrong. Always let them finish saying what they have to say. Allow them to get it off their chest, blow off that steam; and once that's out of their system and they see you're interested and concerned about them, your chances of penetrating their minds and closing the sale are increased substantially.

Then there's Ivan Indecisive. You know about Ivan— who wanted to start up a procrastinators club but decided to wait until later. Ivan simply can't make a decision. He takes a pep pill to get charged up to do something, and then mixes it with Valium so if nothing happens it won't bother him. These people are everywhere.

The way to deal with Ivan is to win his confidence, which you do as I repeatedly implore—by being the right kind of person, honest and sincere. Demonstrate considerable empathy. Move to his side of the table. Let him know you're on his side. Reassure him that he is making the right move. Your own conviction and belief that your product is what he should buy will be the determining factor. Remember, he's having trouble deciding if he should buy. If you have any doubts that you should sell, you can rest assured that he won't buy. Push him, be firm and confident.

Handle objections, using them as closing opportunities.

I close this chapter with this analogy. The sales professional is like a football player. A professional player is interested in running toward the goal post. He understands thoroughly that he can have all the offers he wants. He can get all the appointments he wants. He can make all the plays he wants. But until a football player catches the winning throw or carries the ball across the end zone or kicks the winning field goal, he doesn't know victory.

And until the salesperson takes advantage and capitalizes on closing opportunities, he or she is never going to be successful in the world of selling.

So very many salespeople have come to me and said, "You know, Zig, I can do everything but close. I know how to get prospects. I know how to set up appointments. I know how to handle objections. I can do everything but close." Well what they're really saying is, "I don't know how to sell," because until you close, you're nothing but a conversationalist. You need to know how to handle objections and use them as closing opportunities.

This chapter provided exactly how to do that. Read it again, absorb the information, and then go out there and score!

NOTE

1. Proverbs 18:13 paraphrased.

CHAPTER 9

THE CLOSING

Many years ago, or so the story goes, a fox and a rabbit were having a cool one in the local pub and the fox was doing a considerable amount of talking. He bragged, "You know, I have so many ways to get away from the hounds if any of them would come after me. I could either scoot up into the attic real quick or I could hop out of here and go down to the creek and lose them in the water. Or I could, for that matter, double track and back-track several times. I could lose them a dozen different ways, even go up a tree. There's no way they'd ever get me."

The rabbit said, "Well, I'm afraid I can't do all of those things. If the hounds would come after me, all I could do is just run like a scared rabbit."

About that time, the baying of the hounds were heard reasonably close by.

The fox said, "Now, what should I do? Should I go up and hide in the attic or run to the stream and jump in and confuse them or should I go out and backtrack a few times or climb up a tree...."

While the fox was trying to make up his mind, the hounds came and ate him. Of course, the rabbit didn't know all of those things so the minute he heard the hounds, he just ran like a scared rabbit to safety.

So what am I saying by telling that story? It is better to know one or two or three good closes and use them professionally than to know fifty closes and not use any of them.

But don't you take too much comfort in what I just said because the professional, the real professional, will learn a number of closes so well that each becomes an innate, subliminal, instinctive part of a personal repertoire so that he or she can use them when needed.

Closing is an attitude— and believers are closers.

Closing is an attitude and I want to begin this chapter by saying that believers are closers. Now, what do I mean by that? Several years ago I spoke at the national convention for one of the major life insurance companies on the West Coast. Their top people from all over the country attended, along with their spouses. There were about 2,000.

One morning I was having breakfast with the president and we got to talking. He intrigued me by saying he could take any 100 of his salespeople and provided they had been selling for at least one year, he could without checking a single record as far as their sales were concerned, tell me within five percentage points of what the entire group would produce for the year.

He said, "Zig, all I have to do is look at the amount of life insurance they carry on their own life and then I can predict within five points of what they were going to sell, because the depth of their belief in the product determines their success in the sale of the product."

What I heard loud and clear was that if you're selling Ford automobiles, you ought to be driving a Ford. If you're selling Chevys, you ought to drive a Chevy. When you believe in your product, you will use that product. Now I don't necessarily believe that if you sell 747s, you have to own one, but you sure enough must know everything there is to know about it. I'm certain you understand what I'm saying—that within reason, your belief ought to include yourself and your family.

"IT COSTS TOO MUCH."

Now let's look at some closes or techniques that will produce business at the time you really need it—and in most cases that's going to be right now.

Many times a prospect will say to you, "Well, your product costs too much." In this case, a simple question is helpful to overcome that objection, "Mr. Prospect, wouldn't you agree that it's hard to pay too much for something you really want?"

It's an amazing fact that if you're selling a low-ticket item, a lot of times that question really sets the prospect to thinking and will often say, "Well, I never thought about it that way and I really do like it." Now, if you're selling an expensive item, that question will get their mind to thinking in the right direction, which is the first step toward the close.

Sometimes, though, they will still come back and say, "Well, it just costs too much." And then as we often do, we respond with a question, "Wouldn't you agree, Mr. Prospect, that it's better to invest more than you planned instead of less than you should? If you invest more than you planned, you're talking about pennies. If you invest less than you should and it won't do the job, then you've wasted it all."

For example, when our son was six years old, we went to the store to buy him a bicycle. At the time, the price of a Schwinn bicycle was $64.95. Now, 65 bucks for a bicycle for a six-year-old wasn't practical, knowing he would be learning to ride and all the scrapes and such that entails. So we went to the economy bicycle shop and found a really neat little bicycle for just $34.95. That price was considerably less so we bought it.

A couple of months later when we went to get new handlebars, fortunately the bicycle was still in warranty. It didn't cost us anything. A month or two later though, we went back to get more new handlebars and this time we had to dig up $4.50 more. About six weeks later, the sprocket apparatus completely came unzipped, the whole bit, and by the time they got through with that, it was $15 and change.

About a month later, the bearings in the front wheel came unzipped and we took it back again. This time I said, "No way" to the cost of repair. At that point, I had invested $54.45 in that little bicycle. Our son actually rode that bicycle, not counting the downtime, about six months. The cost of that bicycle was $9 per month.

So, we went and bought a Schwinn bicycle and he actively rode that bicycle for about five years. He play-rided it an additional five years. By that I mean he made a dirt bike out of it and he and a couple of his buddies, boys much too big for it, had a ball on that little bicycle for ten years. The only additional expenses involved were for a couple of tires, which had nothing to do with the quality of the bicycle. When you put your pencil to it, that Schwinn bicycle cost us *$6.50 per year* for its cost.

On the other hand, the price of the less expensive bicycle was $34.95, initially. But the cost of that bicycle was *$9 a month.*

When I use this example when selling, I then look at the prospect and simply say, "Now, Mr. Prospect, *price* is one time. *Cost* spans a product's lifetime. A lot of people can beat us on price—but nobody can beat us on cost." Obviously you want to make certain that statement is true.

I continue, "Now because of that fact, I know you're most concerned with cost, aren't you? So it's simply a matter of working out the details. When would you like to start saving this money? Shall we put it on this program or this plan?"

THE GRANDDADDY CLOSE

Closing can, should, and often is simply a routine follow-through procedure. The following is one you may want to consider using.

When I started my sales career, this close was known as the Granddaddy Close, but I met a young sales trainer in Oregon who identified it as the Disclosure Close.

Here's the scene. You have demonstrated the product, the goods, or the services. And at this point you need to communicate to the prospect exactly what the terms are. A lot of people don't buy because they don't really understand what the offer is. That sounds strange, but many times I really don't understand whether it's 12 payments at $18 or 18 payments at $12. They don't understand what they get with this particular price breakdown and what they get with the other one. So when I mention disclosure, I'm really talking about clarification in a lot of ways and how you lead into it and explain to the prospect how it works.

So now you have your materials out, your order book is handy, and you say, "You know, Mr. and Mrs. Prospect, Uncle Sam enters our lives in a lot of different ways. Some of them are good and some of them not quite so good. One of the things the government did a few years ago, we think is excellent. They require that all companies in our business and in this industry reveal to each customer, the exact terms of the transaction—all the 'hidden' charges. Legitimate companies are delighted to do that. Our company decided to take it one step further. Instead of just revealing to our customers all of the terms, we are required to reveal to every person we talk with exactly what the offer is, written out in black and white."

Now you've just set the stage for writing the order. Then you say to your prospect, "For example, the serial number, our product number we've been talking about is order number 98." Then you write #98 on an order form. "Now the retail value of this is 399.95." When I write this number, I leave off the dollar sign on purpose. "Now, the shipping and handling on this particular order is $20. And that brings it to 419.95. Uncle Sam, as you know, steps into the picture along with the state and they extract

157

an additional $30. So the total price is 449.95." I don't write any names on the order form at this point.

"NOW WAIT A MINUTE."

Along about now, the prospect may say, "Wait a minute. I didn't say I was going to buy anything." Then you can honestly and legitimately look at the prospect and say, "Well, of course you didn't. As a matter of fact, Mr. Prospect, I don't believe anyone would ever decide to buy something or not to buy something until they have enough information or facts to make the decision. So all I'm doing is giving you the exact offer our company has." The response is almost always, "Oh, okay."

Then I say, "But let me ask you a question. *If,* "I strongly emphasize this word, *"If* you were to go ahead with this, would it be more convenient to handle it on our $20 each month deposit program or would you prefer the 60-day cash plan?"

You've just closed on an alternate of choice and a lot of times they repeat it back, "Well, *if,* now I did say *if,* I were to go ahead and get it, I'd have to have it at the $20 deposit each month."

Then we move into another alternate of choice, which really involves a minor decision. A lot of times a minor decision will carry the major decision. I say, "One thing I should mention, Mr. Prospect, is with this particular order, you have a couple of options. You can, for example, choose this electric keyboard to go with it or it might be that you would prefer this entire set of cassettes to reinforce it. Which would you prefer?" You could offer a different item like a knife sharpener or a cleaning brush, "Which would"—the strong word in this case is "would."

If they actually choose an option, say, "Well, I suppose I would like this particular option," then you simply take them into the process one more step. "In getting this, would it make any difference whether the deposits fell on the first or the 15th or would the 25th would be better?"

They may say, "It doesn't really matter. How about the 25th?"

Then you can obviously say, "This is Mr. and Mrs. John Q. Prospect, right?"

Sales trainees often say, "Well, Ziglar, does that kind of stuff really work?"

"No, not all the time." But one of the good things about this type of close is that no one is going to buy anything they don't want. This particular approach clarifies what the offer is up front.

On so many occasions after I cover the figures, then fifteen or twenty minutes later the prospect, having thought about it as we go through other details, says, "Now how much and how long did you say those payments would be? And when would the first one be due?" They have gone back through the process in their mind and you're still in the sales ballgame.

I believe the Disclosure Close is very significant.

WHEN TO CLOSE

The question often comes up, "When should I try to close?" My answer is always, "You close early, close often, and then close late. But don't ever forget—never close or attempt to close until you've established value."

Little things make a big difference in whether or not we're going to make a sale. For example, a manufacturer's rep firm just outside of Chicago secured a major line to sell because the company answered incoming telephone calls by saying, "Good morning! It's a great day!" Several other firms were in competition, everything else seemed to be equal, but the president of the company said, "This telephone greeting is what made the difference with us."

A seemingly small, incidental detail can make a huge difference.

I'll never forget several years ago, for example, I was calling on a firm to sell sales training. The size of the order I was seeking was $18,000. That was their proposal. There were four guys involved who were enthused about what we were doing and they definitely were interested in buying. They said, "We're going to talk it over, weigh it, evaluate, and then we'll get in touch with you."

I kind of smiled and said, "In other words, just as soon as you get around to it, you'll get back to me."

They said, "Yes, we will. You can absolutely count on it. When we get around to it, we are definitely going to buy."

At that time, my business card was a little unusual. It was round and on one side was my name and address, on the other side was T U I T. I pulled four cards out of my pocket and handed one to each of the four guys. I simply said, "Well, gentlemen, I know that you're men of integrity and when you say you're going to do something as soon as you get around to it, I know going to do so. Here's your round tuit." They laughed uproariously and gave me the order.

Now you might say, "Ziglar, you got to be kidding me, you mean they bought because you used a round tuit?" No, that's not the reason they bought. The reason they bought is simply because they were sold on what we were doing and they fully intended to buy and this was kind of a humorous way to move them over into the purchase column. As I say, it is oftentimes a little thing that makes a difference in whether you get it or don't get it.

THE SUBTLE CLOSING

A good closing is not always recognized, even by those who are "experts" in the field. A case in point follows.

We built a wonderful home at Holly Lake, which is 120 miles east of where we live in Dallas. That's where we go to do our writing. We were excited about that home—it turned out beautifully. The "great room" has a 30-foot ceiling. With a ceiling like that there is a lot of wall space.

One day we were down at the lake and our builder and his wife, an interior designer, came by and she just happened to have a large, beautiful wall rug with her. She said, "Zig, I've been thinking about that big empty wall in your home. I believe this would really enhance the appearance of that whole room." Well, because she decorates beautiful hotels all across the country, this rug she was presenting to the redhead and me wasn't exactly dime store merchandise. When she told us what the investment would be, I didn't exactly jump up and down and say, "Whoopee!"

In fact I said, "I don't know about that, Joyce."

She said, "Well, Bill's with me, and how about I have him just go ahead and hang it, because it might fit and it might not fit. But you let it hang there a couple of days and then you'll know."

"Well, that's fine. That makes sense to me."

So they put up the wall rug on the wall. Three hours later during my jog, all of a sudden it hit me what she had done to me. One of the oldest of the best sales tactics! And I'm sure you surmised that the wall rug is still hanging there years later.

INTEGRITY—THE MOST IMPORTANT FACTOR

I believe the most important factor as a closer is the integrity of the salesperson. This might shock you but I do believe there are occasions when your integrity will prevent you from making a sale.

Let me give you a specific example.

One Christmastime, we were shopping for a bicycle for our son. We walked into a store and the owner was talking to a grandmother who had her grandson with her. As she showed him an ad for a bicycle, she said, "This is the bicycle I want. A little boy across the street got this one. I'm going to get it for my grandson. Do you have this bicycle?"

The owner looked at the ad and said, "Yes, we have this exact bicycle. But, ma'am, your grandson is too small for this bicycle. He can't reach the pedals. He needs a smaller bike."

"Oh no," she said, "I want that one. I want the best you got. I want one just like little boy across the street has."

The owner said, "Well now, ma'am, the smaller one is exactly like the bigger one. Same quality, same price, same everything. But it's smaller to fit your grandson."

She said, "Absolutely not. I have to have one exactly like the little boy's across the street."

The owner again said, "Ma'am, that bicycle would be dangerous. Your grandson cannot touch the pedals. If he gets out in the street, he could possibly lose control. There could be a tragic accident."

She said, "I want what I want or I won't get anything at all."

The owner looked at her and said, "Ma'am, this is probably going to shock you, but I cannot sell you that bicycle. I couldn't sleep at night knowing that there was a chance that your grandson would lose control of this someday and maybe get injured. I can't sell you the bicycle."

Incredibly, the grandmother turned around and walked away in an absolute huff.

Now you might ask, "Ziglar, do you really take your integrity that far?" You bet I do. And you should take your integrity that far too.

Since then, we've had occasions to buy other items in that bicycle shop. I would actually send my son or my granddaughters in there with a signed check, amount left open, made out to that store, and say to them, "You buy from him. I know he will do exactly what is right."

That's the way you build a career.

EMPHASIZE THE POSITIVE

Everything really boils down to selling. For example, you're unemployed and looking for a job. You're asked that same old familiar question, "What is your experience?" If you say, "I've been an engineer for twenty-two years, but I don't really have any experience in this department," your chances of getting that job are greatly diminished.

But if you can honestly look at that individual and say, "I have twenty-two years of experience arriving at work every day on time and giving honest effort throughout each day. I have twenty-two years of experience telling the truth. I have twenty-two years of experience knowing that my job depends on the profitability of the company, so I work in such a way that ensures your profitability, not because I'm such a good guy but because I want the security of the job.

"I have twenty-two years of experience getting along well with my coworkers. I have twenty-two years of experience having a winning attitude. Now as far as technical expertise, I have twenty-two years of experience learning, and I'm a good student. And, sir, I believe that's the kind of experience you need in your company. I can start immediately or would next week work into your plans better?"

Yeah, I truly do believe everything is selling, and I believe that with the right words and above all being the right person, you can close more sales—moving you upward by selling your way to the top.

CHAPTER 10

SUCCESSFUL SELLING SECRETS

On average, in the next 24 hours your prospect's heart beats 103,689 times. His blood travels 168,000 miles. His lungs inhale 23,240 times. He'll eat three and a half pounds of food. He'll exercise only 7 million of his 9 billion brain cells. He'll speak 4,800 words of which 3,200 involve something about himself and not a single one will be about you, your products or services—unless you figure out a way to involve him emotionally with your sales situation.

The only way you will get your share of his attention and his words is to use your sales skill and imagination to make yourself part of his world.

PREPARATION

In the world of selling, preparation is often the key. In my early days as a speaker, I had a mentor who at that time was a professor at North Carolina State University. He was conducting sales training seminars for the various chambers of commerce, particularly in the North Carolina area.

I so vividly remember one of the ways he prepared for a sales call. He would empty his wallet and then tie a string around it and attach it to the back bumper of his car. Then he would drag the wallet around town for several days until it absolutely was at the point of falling apart. Then he would put his credit cards and his driver's license and his money back in it and at times he almost had to tie a string around it to keep it together.

When he went into a town to sell a chamber of commerce on sponsoring the seminar—a three evening training presentation for retail merchants—he would always visit three or four of the local stores before he went to see the chamber. At the stores he would buy a neck tie or belt or some item near the counter where they sell wallets. When getting ready to pay, he would intentionally drop the wallet and out would tumble his credit cards, driver's license, money—all the contents would scatter all over the floor.

The people who saw the spectacle were always so nice. The clerks would invariably get down on the floor and help him pick up what dropped. But interestingly enough, not one, no one ever suggested that in addition to the neck tie or belt, maybe just maybe, he needed a new wallet.

Preparation is entirely in the mind.

Sales situations we often run right by is because we're not prepared. I know you heard the story of the woodcutter whose production continued to decrease because he didn't have time to sharpen his ax. Abraham Lincoln put it this way, "If I had to cut a cord of wood and I only had eight hours to do it," he said, "I'd spend the first three hours sharpening my ax."

A lot of times, preparation is entirely in the mind. A good friend from Houston, Texas, sold executive aircraft, and he sold one to Bob Hope. It was a $2 million deal so he obviously took a picture of the transaction. One day he was showing the photograph to a friend of his and the friend said, "When did you make the sale?"

"Four months ago."

The guy said, "Now, I know better than that. You made that sale just last week."

"No. Four months ago is when I conceived the idea of selling the aircraft to Bob Hope—that's when I made the sale. *Not* selling was not an option. It was not an alternative. I planned it carefully. I visualized it. I took all of the steps needed, and missing the sale just simply was not an option."

That's professional selling. My friend sold very, very successfully for more than a decade, and with the application of some of the following principles, his success moved forward at a much faster rate.

IMAGINATION

Sometimes imagination is the key in closing the sale. When I was in the insurance business, one evening during a presentation I wasn't really making any progress. I had covered the standard objections. I had answered the questions. The man could give me no legitimate reason for not buying, and yet I was no closer to the sale than I had been when I walked in the door.

So kind of in desperation, truthfully, I reached up and grabbed this imaginative thought. I said, "Well, Mr. Prospect, perhaps I've been showing you the wrong program. Maybe what you need is our new 29-day agreement. Let me explain this agreement. It gives you the same identical face amount of insurance. The retirement benefits are exactly the same and you have been very clear that these are your first two considerations, first for the protection of the family and second for your later use yourself."

I continued, "Also you get waiver of premium with this one and you also get the double indemnity in the event the death is accidental. And one of the beautiful things about this 29-day agreement is the fact that your monthly investment is only 50 percent as much as it is on the other agreement. Would that suit your needs better?"

The man kind of grinned and said, "Well it'd sure fit my pocket book better. Now, what is this 29-day bit?"

"Well, that means you are covered 29 days out of every month and the company will let you choose the two days you don't wish to be covered, or the one day. You might want to choose a weekend." I paused a bit and then said, "Nah, you're probably at home on the weekend and that's the most dangerous place of all." I really had to work at not smiling or laughing while telling him all that.

Then I got real serious and said, "You know, Mr. Prospect, in all reality, in fairness, if you were to run me out of here at this moment, I could understand because you see I'm making light of something that is very, very serious—the protection and security of your family. Now to put your mind at ease, let me say this, there isn't an insurance commissioner in the world who would approve the sale of any such contract as what I just described. No way. I know what you were thinking as I presented it to you. You were thinking to yourself, *With my luck, something would happen to me on that one or two days each month that I'm not covered.* I simply used this method to alert you to the fact that if you would not leave your family unprotected one or two days out of the month, there is no way you are going to fail to protect your family the 365 days that are in the year."

I continued, seeing I had his attention, "Now, the beautiful thing, Mr. Prospect, about the program you and I have been talking about it is that it covers you 24 hours a day, seven days out of the week, regardless of where you are and regardless of what you're doing. And in reality, that's the kind of coverage you want for your family, isn't it?"

It's amazing what an impact that had. All I had done was dramatize his situation. I've used this approach on a tremendous number of prospects and they have responded in very favorable ways.

You need to adapt that to your own sales situation.

IMAGINATION, CONTINUED

This next one also is an insurance example, but as you'll see, it can easily be adapted to whatever business you're in.

When I was selling insurance for a particular company, we followed a two-part sales approach. We gathered basic information during an interview, formulated an appraisal of the family needs, then our people put the proposal together, and we'd go back for the presentation.

There was a substantial amount of time and effort involved, and the final presentation generally took about 45 minutes. Counting drive time and preliminary preparation, there were about two and a half hours for each call. So, each call was significant.

Something that used to bug the life out of me—to tell you the truth it made me mad—was the fact that many times after making a presentation the prospect would say, "Well, Mr. Ziglar, you obviously know we need the insurance. We recognize that. But I'm a little embarrassed that I permitted you to come back. See, my wife's second cousin has a boyfriend whose neighbor's cousin has an uncle whose son is in college and his roommate's best friend's brother is in the life insurance business. And if we bought, we'd have to buy from him."

Now, obviously, it wasn't quite that convoluted, but it was bad enough that they knew and I knew and they knew that I knew that they weren't going to buy any insurance from anybody if they didn't do business with me. People are inclined along those lines. And so I knew I had to come up with something that would help me overcome that objection, which I heard too regularly.

And then I thought of an idea as a direct result, incidentally of reading Frank Bettger's book, *How I Raised Myself from Failure to Success in Selling*.[1] I had read that book ten years earlier. It is still a classic in the world of selling and one of the major reasons I spend so much time selling you on the idea of growing and learning.

So I came up with an idea, and the next time a prospect hit me with that friend-of-a-cousin-of-an-in-law line, I smiled all over. I couldn't wait. I almost planted the objection myself, as a matter of fact.

When a prospect said something like that, my response was, "Well, Mr. Prospect, I'm sure the individual you're speaking about is a fine person. And if they are licensed in this state, they're okay. And I know if their company is licensed here, and obviously it is, that's fine. There's nothing at all wrong with either that individual, so far as I know, or certainly not with that company—but I can do something for you that no other insurance man alive can do for you."

"Oh, what's that?"

"Mr. Prospect, I can marry you."

And with that, I reached down and I pulled from my briefcase a marriage certificate. Then I read the wording on the beautifully printed parchment paper:

Certificate of Marriage

> Isaac Ziglar on this day in (I'd already typed in the date), agree to the marriage between myself and John and Mary Smith. (I'd already typed in their name) And by this agreement, Zig Ziglar

agrees to stay abreast of all the trends in the industry as it relates to social security and other programs, which directly relate to the lives and fortunes of John and Mary Smith. I agree to be available in time of need. John and Mary Smith agree to give Zig Ziglar the privilege of earning the right to serve.

Then I say, "Now, all it needs, Mr. and Mrs. Prospect, is your okay right here. And the marriage will be official."

The response was absolutely amazing. Mostly hilarious. The prospects usually laugh and say, "Oh boy. Now Mr. Ziglar, is this legitimate? You're not going to get us involved with the law, are you?"

I smile and say, "No, I've cleared it with the governor of the state and the insurance commissioner says it's fine. I even got approval from my brother-in-law."

And just about always the husband turns to his wife and says, "Honey what do you think about it? You want to marry this fella?"

She said, "Well, he wants to marry us both and he looks like an all right guy to me. Why don't we do it?"

And the old boy says, "Yeah, let's go ahead and take a spin," as he signs the certificate while laughing. But a funny thing happened on the way to the bank. I never once got the okay on the marriage agreement, that I didn't get the okay on the application for the insurance.

It really was a trial close. Wasn't it? Your imagination really does help sometime.

Preparation and imagination are a winning combination!

THE TENNIS RACKET CLOSE

More often than not, your imagination is a consistent and reliable standby that produces business. I'm going to tie two closes together here to show you what I mean—the Tennis Racket and the Ben Franklin. The first one you might not have heard of, the second one you undoubtedly have heard of if you've been in selling very long at all.

Sometimes we're involved in a sale situation where two people are going to be making the decision, could be two business partners or a husband and wife, and they're kind of tossing the decision back and forth. One may say to the other, "Well, what do you think?"

The other person says, "Well, it's up to you."

"No, you're the one who has the expertise in this area."

"Well, you're the one who will use it." And back and forth they go, batting the ball from one to the other.

What they're really saying is, "You decide." "No, you decide." "No, you decide." And that can mean one of three things: (1) both want to buy but don't want to make the commitment; or (2) neither want to buy and don't want to make the commitment; or (3) one person wants it and the other doesn't, but neither wants to voice their preference.

When they bat that decision ball back and forth more than twice, particularly between a husband and wife, it's been my experience that one will then knock it out of the ballpark—generally the husband. He'll smile ever so pleasantly and then say, "Well, I'm sure that we're going to end up getting it, but she can't make up her mind." Bless his heart.

Now as a salesperson who wants to close the deal, how do you handle that? Well, when the ball is passed across that net a couple of times, what you can do is literally hold up your hand and say, "Scuse me," (in some parts of the country, they would say, "Excuse me," but that's wrong. It's scuse me.) "maybe I shouldn't say this, but I'm going to. I believe, Mr. and Mrs. Prospect, that neither one of you should make this decision. The reason I say that is simply because you are both emotionally involved, and regardless of what you decide, if you decide yes, then later one of you might say, 'Well, I'll tried to get you not to do that.' If you say no, the other one might say, 'Well, if you had got that thing, we wouldn't be having this trouble.'

177

When you're emotionally involved, it isn't a good time to make a decision. Let me be so bold as to suggest that instead of letting emotion decide, why not let the actual facts make the decision?"

THE BEN FRANKLIN CLOSE

Now you've set the scene for the Ben Franklin Close.

I looked at both prospects and said, "Here's what I mean by letting the facts make the decision. Many years ago, one of the wisest men our country ever produced was Benjamin Franklin. When Franklin was confronted with a very difficult decision, he would take a sheet of paper and draw a line down the middle. At the top of one column he wrote the word 'For' and at the top of the other side he wrote 'Against.' Then Mr. Franklin would list the reasons for doing something. Now, for example, one of the reasons you want to go ahead and make this move is because you really like the product. You like it and you want it."

Now, let me tell you something, my fellow salesperson friend, people are going to buy what they like and what they want. They'll work at figuring out a way, you might have to come up with some creative financing for it, but they're going to work at buying what they like and what they want.

So, get out a piece of paper and while they watch you, draw a line down the middle and write "For" at the top of one column, and the word "Against" at the top of the second column. Then ask the couple why they want to go ahead with the transaction. Write down whatever you and the couple come up with to add to the "For" list. There should be a number of reasons for them to go ahead and buy.

Note: *Don't* put any numbers by each of the reasons. That's important. Do *not* write numbers beside the reasons. Why? You may get involved in a contest with your prospect. When they move to the Against side, one may say, "Well, there are 17 for and 13 against, let me see if I can come up with more." And they may come up with some of the most asinine things you can possibly imagine.

When you and the couple have exhausted all of the positive reasons for moving ahead with the sale, and all have been written in the For column, then say, "There are some reasons why you definitely should not make this move." I feel very strongly about this particular point. You need to list the one or two things that have been dominating the conversation.

If one of the prospects, for example, has been protesting, "We just don't have any money," you need to write that down yourself. Don't wait for them to tell you. If you do, then it has more impact. If they remind you again, it has less impact. If you acknowledge what they have already said, it indicates you've been listening. It indicates you have empathy. It indicates you understand, and people do always want to be understood.

179

So you come up with one or two things that have dominated the conversation. Then don't say another word and let the prospects add to the Against list. Now if you've done your job, you're going to have substantially more Fors than they come up with reasons against.

When they run out of Againsts, then you count them, "Let's see there's one, two, three, four, five, six, seven, eight, nine, ten reasons why you should go ahead." Then you write a 10 and circle it several times. Then say, "There are several reasons not—one, two, three, four, five, six," and you write a big six and circle it.

Then you look directly at the prospects, lower your voice and say, "You know, Mr. and Mrs. Prospect, if all of the people I deal with took this logical approach to making the decision, such as you have, my business would be even more fun. We can have this installed within the week, or if you're really in a hurry, I'll have a service person see you tomorrow afternoon. Which would suit your needs better?"

Now let me stress the point that it is possible the prospect can come up with only one reason against, and you could miss the sale. And I also want to stress that they aren't going to buy it for ten reasons. They going to buy it for one or two reasons. If you can give people one or two very good reasons for buying, like, for example, it will pay for itself or it is more convenient or whatever, your chances of making the sale are dramatically enhanced.

You may be wondering, *Then why list ten and six if they're going to decide only on one or two reasons?* Very simple. It helps to *keep* it sold. When they explain to their friends, relatives, and neighbors why they bought, they will say, "Man, just look at all the reasons why we bought!" You're giving them a logical explanation for it and that is important.

> The fear of loss is greater than the desire for gain.

Always remember to weave into your presentation that the fear of loss is greater than the desire for gain. If in your close you can make it clear that they're going to lose if they don't buy, that's more powerful than just concentrating on the gain if they do buy. The fear of loss is greater than the desire for gain.

THE SIGNATURE CLOSE

I close this chapter with what I honestly believe is the most powerful single sales close I have ever heard. Now that might sound strange because I'm now going to modestly admit that I originated this close. I want to tell you something about the close before I share it with you. This is the close of last resort.

What used to happen to me is that when I got down to the nitty gritty and they have to make the decision, the prospect would say, "Well, I just don't sign anything until _____." (I sleep on it or talk to my husband or talk to my wife or talk to my banker or check with a CPA or whatever.) The truth is in most cases, if they give you lots of excuses including "I'll buy later," in so many instances, they're trying to let you down easily.

But if you really believe the sale is there, why not explore every avenue to make the sale right then? If there is a sale to be made, I believe the Signature Close will get it.

Don't use this close to sell a small $15 or a $50 order. This is something you use on a major purchase. As I share the close with you, I'm going to grossly exaggerate it. I'm going to give you a smorgasbord of things to choose from. But remember, you must *use no more than three* and probably two would be better. Your own comfort zone will dictate which ones you use.

Okay, so the prospect says to you, "I just don't sign anything until…" then they give you the reason or reasons.

You start your answer with the oldest response of them all and tailoring your wording to suit your particular circumstances, "I know exactly how you feel, Mr. Prospect. For years and years and years, I felt the same way, but when I really dug into it and explored the facts I found. I (feel, felt, found) that everything I own or have that has any value at all, I acquired only after I had signed my name. For example, Mr. Prospect, I'm one of those extremely lucky (blessed) men. I've been married for well over forty years and can honestly say I love my wife today infinitely more than I did the day we married in the presence of the minister and some friends and almighty God, I signed my name."

Pause briefly then continue, "I have four beautiful children. They're all mine. But before I could even take them out of the hospital, I had to sign my name. I have a beautiful home. Oh, I love that home with an absolute passion. And I got that home because one day in the presence of the builder, the mortgage lending people, the insurance people, the attorney, and half the city of Dallas, I signed my name. I have an enormous amount of insurance. I've always had lots of insurance because I wanted to make certain that if something happened to me, my wife would not be forced to work, especially if the children were young. I wanted to ensure the fact that my children would have the opportunity to go to college if they wanted to and that my family's standard of living would not suffer just because old dad wasn't around. I got that insurance because on many different occasions, in the presence of a skilled life insurance representative, I signed my name."

Then I said, "I have a number of investments because I want to make absolutely certain that when I reach the point in life when I can no longer do what I'm doing, that

I won't be a burden on anybody. That I can be entirely independent and self-supporting. I was able to do that because on a number of occasions, in the presence of a skilled counselor, I signed my name. As a matter of fact, Mr. Prospect, everything I have that has any value or significance to me at all is mine only because I signed my name.

"And if I'm reading you right, and I believe I am, you're the kind of individual who likes not only to do things in the proper manner and do things for his family and his business, but he likes to make progress at the same time. You can do all of those things right now by signing your name."

And you say absolutely nothing else. Nothing.

I didn't always make the sale with the Signature Close—but I always felt good about it. Now I confess, I felt lots better if I did make the sale, but I always felt good regardless. Why? Because I knew I had done everything I could to get the sale, and to tell the prospect how important it is to me to take care of my family.

Please note that if you've been laughing and kidding and backslapping all the way through the interview, and then try to pull out this serious conversation, I can assure you it's not going to work for you. But if it's a significant product and you've been sincerely concerned that the prospect buys, this one can make a difference.

Yes, I believe skills and techniques are some of the secrets of successful selling that you absolutely must learn and then relearn and update and use all the time. Do those things and you'll have a much richer, more exciting, more rewarding sales career as you sell your way to the top.

NOTE

1. Frank Bettger, *How I Raised Myself from Failure to Success in Selling* (New York: Touchstone/Simon & Schuster, 1992).

CHAPTER 11

SELL YOURSELF ON SELLING

It's an amazing fact that many salespeople are proud of the product they sell, they're proud of the company they represent, they're proud of the income they're enjoying, and they're excited about their future.

But even more amazing is that many salespeople are embarrassed to say, "I sell for a living."

You might be thinking to yourself, *What's the big deal about that?* Well, let me simply say that how you feel about the sales profession plays a major role in the success of your career.

Now we're going to get involved in selling you on your profession. You might say, "Well, that sounds kind of strange, Ziglar. I've been selling twenty (thirty, forty) years, and now you're going to sell me on being a salesperson?"

Yes, because you have an obligation that goes beyond meeting your own needs and the needs of your family. You have an obligation to the profession itself, which has been so good to you.

There has always been a lot of misconceptions about a sales career, so let's explore it and really see what is the sales profession.

SALE—TO SERVE

The very word "sale" is much better and more accurately described by the Norwegian word, *sclje*, which literally means to serve; to sale is to serve. For example, I'm a prospect and you call on me, selling a product I need. If you sell me something that solves my problem, you have helped me get what I want. By providing a product and making a sale, you receive income along with the satisfaction that goes with it. Yes, the word sale and the sales profession really is important.

I'm convinced beyond any doubt that the United States of America is great. And one of the reasons we are so great is because of the salespeople who have made it great.

Many of us believe that the United States is the greatest land on the face of this earth. But that is not because of our geographical size. There are many larger countries than the United States including Russia, China, and Canada. And we're not the greatest because we have the most people—China and India have larger populations. The

US is richly blessed with natural resources nationwide, but other countries are as well. And Japan has been proven to be technologically superior, but the US is right behind them when it comes to technology advancements.

I'm convinced America is great because we're a land of salespeople. Let's explore that statement further.

To begin with, the land was discovered by a salesman. Not by any stretch of imagination could you accuse Christopher Columbus of being a navigator; after all, he was actually looking for India. He missed it by 12,000 miles, yet went back home and told them he had found it.

You might say, "Okay, he wasn't a navigator, but was he a salesman?" Well, let's just look at the facts. Columbus was an Italian in Spain, now that's way out of his territory. He only has one prospect and if he doesn't make the sale, he has to swim home. Now you tell me, was he a salesman or not?

COLUMBUS, AMERICA'S FIRST SALESMAN

Remember the sales call Columbus made to Queen Isabella? My version of the transaction follows: Columbus told the queen the whole story about wanting to find a new trade route to India and would like her financial support. She heard what he said, but she didn't really hear what he was saying. Initially, prospects only hear the price and skim over the benefits.

Isabella only heard the price, so Chris knew he needed to sell her the benefits. He hammered the fact that Spain would beat England and France and Portugal—the world power he had approached and been turned down—as the first to find a shorter route to India. I imagine him saying, "Think of the financial rewards that will come your way if we find it first!" Isabella and King Ferdinand were strong Christians, so Chris also told them, "And we'll be able to spread the gospel over there!" He really sold the benefits and finally the benefits exceeded the price.

Until the benefits exceed the price, a prospect is just a suspect.

Until in the prospect's mind the benefits are more than the price, you don't really have a prospect, you just have a suspect. Now Chris had a prospect, but the prospect has an objection, "Chris, I know it sounds like a good deal, but I don't have any money."

He said, "Look, Izzy..." (I wasn't there so I doubt this is verbatim) "...you have that string of beads around your neck and lots of fancy jewelry, let's take them down to the pawn shop and see if we can finance this deal." Well, it wasn't quite like that, but history books reveal that she indeed did offer to sell her royal jewelry to finance the voyage. It didn't come to that but she and the king did have to do some creative financing for Columbus to make the trip.

Then when the trip started, Columbus had to do some real selling. He had to sell his new, unproven, unorthodox sailing route to the crews of the three ships. Columbus didn't plan his route by using the charts of the day because of the winds. All the other explorers had been sailing due west, which ran directly into strong winds, hitting them head on. As a matter of fact, King John II from Portugal, had just sent out another expedition, trying to find a shorter and safer route to India, and the winds drove him backward.

What Columbus wanted to do is sail south and then later turn westward so the prevailing winds would be at his back. The superstitious, fearful sailors didn't understand and they threatened to mutiny. They were going to throw Columbus overboard—and he had to sell his plan hard. As a matter of fact, the captains of the other two ships— the *Niña* and the *Pinta*—were equally confused and ready to toss Chris into the uncharted waters.

So the three of them got together for a sales meeting. The other captains said, "Chris, our crews are ready to toss us overboard along with you. We can't even depend on our officers. We gotta stop going in the wrong direction and get back on course."

I can only imagine that Columbus sold as he had never sold before in his life. He gave them his best presentation about the winds and the route and then said, "Give me three more days." And they agreed.

Just four hours before the three days expired, the call came forth, "Tierra! Tierra, land ho!" The new land was discovered with only four hours to spare. Christopher Columbus had to do a lot of selling. He had to be very convincing. His conviction led to a major discovery that changed the face of the globe.

Then Columbus made the biggest mistake of his sales career—he didn't service the account. The new land didn't become the United States of Columbus.

SELL AND SERVICE

We became the United States of America because another salesman entered the picture. Amerigo Vespucci came in and serviced the account that Columbus sold.

We were, perhaps, populated by a salesman, Sir Walter Raleigh, who toured the coffee houses of London, educating and selling people on the idea that they should leave the security of their native land and go to the "new world" to find their fortunes in America.

We were freed by a salesman. George Washington has to rate as one of the all-time professionals in the world of selling. He had to sell the merchants and the seamen and the farmers and the lumberjacks and all able-bodied men on going to war against the most powerful nation on earth with the largest army and the largest navy. Washington had to sell them on the preposterous notion that even if they went to war, they wouldn't be paid, and if they lose the war, they'd probably be hung from the closest tree. Can you imagine that presentation?

If you are a recruiter with your company, could you tell a prospective salesperson, "I want to give you a chance, but if you make the sale, there isn't any money to pay you. And if you miss the sale, we're going to shoot you at sunrise." Now *that* would require some heavy-duty persuasion.

FINANCIAL SECURITY

Let's suppose my son came to me and asked, "Dad, what career would you suggest for me if I wanted to feel as secure financially as you do?" I would look my own son right in the eye and say, "Son, get into the profession of selling. That's where security is."

He may then ask, "But Dad, doesn't everyone generally work on a commission in selling? That doesn't seem like a secure income."

"Yes, son, but everybody in life works on a commission."

He may say, "Now, wait a minute. I know the president of your company and I know your secretary, and both get paid an annual salary."

"Yeah, everybody there is on salary, but they're really on commission. I say this simply because anyone who doesn't produce, regardless of whether they are on salary or commission, will be dismissed eventually."

Why do I say selling is a secure career field? You may remember the recession in the mid-1980s. At our company, we only really knew there was a recession because we read about it in the newspapers. The articles reported that the US was in a recession.

Well, our company decided not to join. I've joined a lot of clubs, but not the recession club. Granted, many people lost their jobs during that time. A lot of good people; people who were honest and sincere and conscientious and hardworking and productive. Maybe the flight attendant or the plane's captain; maybe the mail carrier or the postmaster, maybe the school teacher or the principal. But no honest, sincere, dedicated, hardworking salespeople lost their jobs. And if they did, if their company went out of business, they just went down the street and got another sales job.

Selling is the most secure profession in our country today.

There's always a market for somebody who can sell, who's honest and who is hardworking. Business handles recessions one way, we salespeople handle them in an entirely different way. In business, a lot of times when there's a recession they call a very serious, gloomy yet sincere meeting. The top dog may say somberly, "You know what the problem is. I mean, it's tough, but we're going to make it. We'll just simply turn off a few lights. We'll discharge a few people here and there. We'll cut all the corners. We'll tough it out, and we're going to make it. We're going to fight this thing."

On the other hand, salespeople call a meeting and the manager stands up and says, "Now you've heard all this stuff about a recession, but we have a plan. All we have to do is just reduce our sales." Ha! No, of course the manager doesn't say that.

In reality the manager says, "You've been hearing all that baloney about the recession. Well, let me tell you my response to that. We're going to put on training sessions like you've never seen before. We're going to have motivational sessions like you have never seen before. We're going to put on a contest to end all kinds of debt.

195

We at our company are going to sell more and more and more."

Let me ask you a question, my salesperson friend. Which meeting would you rather be sitting in? Remember what I said at the beginning of this book—your business is not good or bad *out there*. It's good or bad right between your own two ears! Your mind is powerful.

FREEDOM

You know why I'm excited about selling? You can start young and you can keep at it until you're 96 or 106, for that matter. What I love about it, though, is the freedom. Every morning you can get up and look in the mirror and say to yourself, "You're such a nice guy or gal...you deserve a raise!" And the board just met! That's exciting to me.

You're the chairman of the board, you're the president, you're the treasury secretary, and yet you're also the janitor. You're the one who decides whether to give yourself a raise or even to lay yourself off, whether to move yourself up or bring yourself down by your decisions and your actions. Nothing regarding your career is subjected to the whims of others.

As salespeople, we are for ourselves, but not by ourselves. In 2018 it was reported that 15 percent of Fortune 500 CEOs started in sales.[1] Selling is fun, it's challenging, it's rewarding. And as Red Motley, *Parade* magazine publisher and former Fuller brush salesman, said so eloquently, "Nothing happens until somebody sells something." *Parade* magazine's circulation reached 10 million after Motley took over; and one of his colleagues said about him, "He's the greatest salesman God ever created."[2]

PERPETUAL EFFECTS OF A SALE

Have you ever wondered or thought about what really *does* happen when you make a sale? Many salespeople don't. Well, let's think about it together now.

First of all, let's examine just one tiny aspect of making a sale and how it positively impacts so many others. A salesperson writes down sale details on a tablet (paper or electronic). Paper starts as a tree that someone planted, then was cut down by another someone, and someone else hauled it to the paper mill where more people ran the machines that grinded the wood chips to collect fiber that produced pulp that was given pressure and dried and created a thin sheet of paper. Hundreds, maybe thousands, of people are involved in manufacturing trees into paper products, and you're one of the individuals paying those people.

But your sale goes even a lot farther than that because of what you do with your income from the sale.

When you make a sale, you make a profit, your manager makes a profit, and hopefully your company makes a profit. I say hopefully because, if the company doesn't make a profit, you may not have a job with that company for very long—they will go out of business.

With your profit you can go to the grocery store and buy a can of beans, some chicken, and a gallon of milk. When you buy those groceries, the store manager keeps track and when the supply gets low, the manager contacts the wholesalers and orders more beans and chicken and milk. The wholesaler in turn contacts the cannery, the chicken farmer, and the dairy farm to order more for the grocery store. You get the picture.

Tracking the beans, the person at the cannery knows how many canned beans there are and when in short supply, the cannery contacts the bean farmer for more beans. The farmer sends the beans and then has to raise more beans to sell. His tractor is worn out so he has to buy a new tractor. The farmer goes to the tractor supply store and says, "Hey, I need a new tractor."

"I have one left," the salesperson replies. After the sale to the farmer, the tractor supply salesperson calls the tractor factory and says, "I just sold the last tractor, so I need to build up my inventory." The factory manager says, "Okay, I'll call the manufacturers to get the iron, copper, plastic, steel, aluminum, lead, zinc, and spark plugs we need to get you more." And the manager proceeds to contact supplies worldwide to secure the products needed to build the tractor.

And all of that happened because one day you got out there and made a sale.

Salespeople keep commerce wheels rolling.

That's what you ought to tell folks. Hundreds of thousands of people in the US and tens of millions worldwide are enjoying their standard of living because you and others like you are out there in the world selling. Because that is a fact, why is it that we don't enjoy the good reputation that we should? Why do some people look down on salespeople?

SELLING THE SALES PROFESSION

I think one basic problem is we've sold our goods, we've sold our services, and we've sold our companies—but we haven't sold our profession. A lot of people think that all salespeople want to do is sell people something they don't need, has no real use, or simply has no value. And many people they think selling is making people buy something they don't even want.

What is the real truth? The role we salespeople play is very important for the world, nation, region, community, family, and you the individual. And we must believe that to be successful.

We need to not only believe it but also spread that word around. We need support through confidence-building organizations such as the sales and marketing clubs, the SWAP clubs (Salesman with a Purpose) and the National Speakers Association. Many of the speakers are outstanding sales trainers; and, after all, you know by now that everyone is a salesperson. Get involved in organizations like that.[3]

We need to inform people about how important the salesperson and the profession really are.

Many years ago, the following poem was written by an unknown author, and I share it with you because I believe it's true to the core:

> I am proud to be a salesman, because more than any other man, I and millions of others like me, built America.

The man who builds a better mouse trap—or a better *anything*—would starve to death if he waited for people to beat a pathway to his door. Regardless of how good or how needed the product or service might be, it has to be sold.

Eli Whitney was laughed at when he showed his cotton gin. Edison had to install his electric light free of charge in an office building before anyone would even look at it. The first sewing machine was smashed to pieces by a Boston mob. People scoffed at the idea of railroads. They thought that traveling even thirty miles an hour would stop the circulation of the blood! McCormick strived for 14 years to get people to use his reaper. Westinghouse was considered a fool for stating he could stop a train with wind. Morse had to plead before 10 Congresses before they would even look at his telegraph.

The public didn't go around demanding these things; they had to be sold!!

They needed thousands of salesmen, trailblazers and pioneers—people who could persuade with the same effectiveness as the inventor could invent. Salesmen took these inventions, sold the public on what these products could do, taught customers how to use them, and then taught businessmen how to make a profit from them.

As a salesman, I've done more to make America what it is today than any other person you know. I was just as vital in your great-great-grandfather's day as I am in yours, and I will be just as vital in your great-great-grandson's day. I have educated more people, created more jobs, taken more drudgery from the laborer's work, given more profits to businessmen, and have given more people a fuller and richer life than anyone in history. I've dragged prices down, pushed quality up, and made it possible for you to enjoy the comforts and luxuries of automobiles, radios, electric refrigerators, televisions, and air-conditioned homes and buildings. I've healed the sick, given security to the aged, and put thousands of young men and women through college. I've made it possible for inventors to invent, for factories to hum, and for ships to sail the seven seas.

How much money you find in your pay envelope next week, and whether in the future you will enjoy the luxuries of prefabricated homes, stratospheric flying of airplanes, and new world of jet propulsion and atomic power, depends on me. The loaf of bread you bought today was on a baker's shelf because I made sure that a farmer's wheat got to a mill, that the mill made wheat into flour, and that the flour was delivered to your baker.

Without me, the wheels of industry would come to a grinding halt. And with that, jobs, marriages, politics, and freedom of thought would be a thing of the past. I AM A SALESMAN, and I'm proud and grateful that as such, I serve my family, my fellow man, and my country.

NOTES

1. Parth Misra, "5 Reasons Every Entrepreneur Should Start in Sales," *Entrepreneur,* July 16, 2018; https://www.entrepreneur.com/article/315650; accessed May 22, 2021.

2. James Barron, "Author H. Motley Dies at 83," *The New York Times,* May 31, 1984; https://www.nytimes.com/1984/05/31/obituaries/arthur-h-motley-dies-at-83-parade-magazine-publisher.html; accessed May 22, 2021.

3. This link lists several Sales Professional Associations & Organizations: https://jobstars.com/sales-professional-associations-organizations/; accessed May 23, 2021.

ABOUT
THE AUTHOR

Zig Ziglar (1926–2012) was one of America's most influential and beloved encouragers and believers that everyone could be, do, and have more. He was a motivational speaker, teacher, and trainer who traveled extensively delivering messages of humor, hope, and encouragement. His appeal transcended age, culture, and occupation. From 1970 until 2010, Zig traveled more than five million miles around the world sharing powerful life-improvement messages, cultivating the energy of change.

Zig Ziglar wrote more than thirty celebrated books on personal growth, leadership, sales, faith, family, and success. He was a committed family man, dedicated patriot, and an active church member. His unique delivery style and powerful presentations earned him many honors, and today he is still considered one of the most versatile authorities on the science of human potential.